America: Lost in Place

America: Lost in Place

Musings at 70+

Dr. Joe Brickner

Sunne Pharms Publishing
Shawnee, Kansas

Edited by: William Toepfer

Copyright © 2022 by Dr. Joseph L. Brickner.

All rights reserved. No part of this publication may be reproduced, stored in a retrieval system, or transmitted in any form or by any means: electronic, recording, photocopying, mechanical, or otherwise without the prior written permission of Sunne Pharms LLC Publishing, P.O. Box 3275, Shawnee, Kansas 66203.

ISBN 978-1-7354315-2-9   (Paperback)
ISBN 978-1-7354315-3-6   (eBook)
ISBN 978-1-7354315-4-3   (Hardback)
Library of Congress Control Number: 2022912135

Library of Congress Publisher's Cataloging-in-Publication Data
Names: Brickner, Joe, author.
Title: America: lost in place : musings at 70+ / Dr. Joe Brickner.
Description: Shawnee, KS : Sunne Pharms Publishing, 2022.
Identifiers: LCCN 2022912135 (print) | ISBN 978-1-7354315-2-9
    (paperback) | ISBN 978-1-7354315-3-6 (ebook)
Subjects: LCSH: United States--History--1945- | United States--Social
    conditions--1945- | Faith. | Liberty. | Families. | BISAC: HISTORY
    / United States / 20th Century.
Classification: LCC E741 .B37 2022 (print) | LCC E741 (ebook) | DDC
    973.9--dc23.

Website: www.drjoebrickner.com

Dedication

This book is dedicated to all those "influencers" who molded me over the years, especially early in my life:

- My Aunt Helen Brickner Korte, who taught me how to pray
- My grandpa and grandma, Joe and Lizzy Brickner, who taught me the value of hard work
- My mother, Lucy Brickner, who taught me right from wrong
- My 6th and 7th grade teacher, Sr. Mary Roselma, who taught me how to have fun learning
- My high school principal, Fr. E.C. Herr, who taught me to be resilient
- My high school basketball coach and history teacher, Bill Clark, who taught me the value of a sense of humor
- My college assistant basketball coach, Tom Colwell, who taught me to never give up
- My corporate management mentor, Don George, who taught me to treat people with dignity

Podcast

Dr. Brickner also hosts a weekly podcast called:

"Building with Brick: Foundational Wisdom on Coaching, Careers and Christ"

The video and audio podcast links can be found at
www.drjoebrickner.com.

Acknowledgements

This, my second book, was much easier to write than my first one. Yes, going through the experience of writing a first book helped ease the burden of composing a second. The first book contained a lot of emotional issues that I had to face before I could complete it. There are emotional issues in this book also, but they are different. For the most part, my memories of "the good old days" are good memories. We did not have a lot of money or material things as I grew into manhood, but the family ties and the mentors and friends I had were wonderful. Therefore, it was easy to write about those good times. What was not easy was admitting that things today in America are not as good as they were. Change is normally good as time progresses, but not so in this case. We can do more things quicker and more accurately today, but the purpose is not as noble. We have lost a portion of integrity in this American experiment, and that is both sad and unfortunate.

I would not be able to look back on my past so fondly without the contributions of those people I dedicated this book to in the Dedication section. As you age you look back on the influencers in your life and sometimes you surprise yourself with the names that pop up. They are people who at the time did not seem to have had much of an influence on you at all. But later, you reflect on why you feel or think or act the way you do, and that teacher, coach, relative, or boss's face appears. Those are the names I listed in the Dedication section and must acknowledge here as the shapers of me personally.

As far as helping me with writing this book, I'll first thank my wife, Connie. She is my biggest cheerleader and my biggest critic. If I were a Roman warrior, she would be the one behind my chariot reminding me that I am mortal and must remain humble. She'd also be intermittently telling me to "kick their ___" and reminding me that "you got this." That is her attitude when she reviews my books.

I'd also like to again thank my good friend, Bill Toepfer. He not only reviewed the book, he also edited it for me. He is someone who I know I can trust – he will tell me things I need to hear and make me consider all alternatives. In fact, he was the one who came up with the final title for the book. I was going to simply call it "Musings at 70+" but he suggested that "America: Lost in Place" would better reflect the content. He then, graciously, suggested that using my original title as a subtitle would still convey the idea that this was a reflection of a lifetime of experiences. I think he was right.

Mike Tharp, a former college teammate and an extremely successful journalist for some of the most prestigious media giants in the world, once again agreed to edit this book, as he did my first book. To have a professional the caliber of Mike providing guidance is invaluable. However, he is facing extremely serious health issues and was unable to do the word-by-word editing that he would normally do. He was on my Editorial Board and, being the warrior he is, he still gave me his best shot. That is the type of friend and professional he is.

Charlie Johnston, who wrote the Foreword for me, has been an inspiration. His jovial presence and hope-filled attitude keeps me going. He helps keep my focus on God, even when the world looks like it is headed for hell!

Finally, I am simply going to lift this last paragraph out of my first book's "Acknowledgments" section. It pertains to our Creator:

> "I want to thank God. He has been so good to me for 70+ years. He always made sure we had enough to cover the necessities, and he put people in my pathway that had such a positive influence on me. He's been there when I have been down, and He has been there when I've been up. He has allowed me to have a wonderful spiritual life and blessed me with a wonderful family."

Table of Contents

Introduction 1

Chapter 1 - The Way We Were 7

Chapter 2 - Simple Times, Simple Formula 11

Chapter 3 - The Three R's 15

Chapter 4 - Advanced Education 21

Chapter 5 - Jobs and Careers 27

Chapter 6 – Money 31

Chapter 7 – Shopping 35

Chapter 8 - Entertainment 41

Chapter 9 – Comedy 53

Chapter 10 – Travel 57

Chapter 11 - Exercise & Health 61

Chapter 12 – Healthcare 67

Chapter 13 - Race Relations 73

Chapter 14 - Family 81

Chapter 15 – Faith 85

Chapter 16 – Environment 89

Chapter 17 – Mass Media 95

Chapter 18 – Government 99

Chapter 19 – Freedom 103

Chapter 20 – Summary Analysis 109

Chapter 21 – Conclusion 115

Chapter 22 – Recommendations 121

About the Author 129

Foreword

Joe Brickner is a man who wears many hats. He is a husband, father, and an exuberantly sunny and engaging friend. Professionally, he is a Doctor of Business Administration who has used those skills as both a corporate executive and a professor of business administration. At heart, though, he is a coach. For 12 years he was head men's basketball coach at Benedictine College in Atchison, Kansas, where he taught business administration.

A coach is many things, including mentor, friend, and motivator of those he is charged with leading. To be successful a coach must know his sport and how it has been played successfully in the past. He must know the plays that work and in what situations they work. He must look hard at how even the most successful tactics have failed in the past. He must know what tactics are best suited to what circumstances. It is a kaleidoscope of knowledge he must have to adapt capably to the kaleidoscope of circumstances he and his team will face. He must be intimate with the past to understand how to deal with the present.

The coach must know his team's strengths and weaknesses in the present. Not only that, he must know each of his players and understand what motivates them and how they learn. He must know when to offer an encouraging word and when to give a swift kick to the rear, not out of either sentimentality or irritability, but to get the best out of each of his players and the team. He must help them first to discover their own strengths, to see that they are capable of more than they realized and then to apply those strengths to the contest at hand. Even more, he must show them how to meld their skills together seamlessly so that their ultimate achievement transcends the sum of any individual talent. To do this, he must assess the team and its players with rigorous clarity with the heart to show them how to find the best in themselves – and each other. He must take an unvarnished view of the present to build a workable vision of future success.

The coach must be a visionary. He must use his intimate knowledge of the past and his clear-eyed assessment of the people he has to forge a path to victory and achievement. This is not a task for people who are always yearning for the ideal team. It is a calling for the man who can look at what is and figure out how to win with what he has. It is a job for a man whose feet are firmly planted on the ground but whose head not only soars, but also inspires all around him to soar with him, transcending their own limitations.

Joe uses all he has learned as a husband, father and friend to write this book. He applies the skills he has owned as a businessman and a professor to flesh the book out. Most of all, this is Coach Brickner writ large, recalling who we were, what we are, and what we can be together.

The nostalgic elements of the book moved me. Joe and I are of the same generation, if a decade apart. He grew up in the 50's and 60's; I grew up in the 60's and 70's. He was a farm boy; I was a suburban boy. We both lived in a culture of individual responsibility, one in which we were each called to judge those around us with charity and ourselves with rigor. The morality our parents instilled in us was not based on relentlessly looking for the flaws in others, but rigorously demanding the best of ourselves. Though Joe's family was of modest means, he had the benefit of growing up in a community and time that was rich in standards of morality and family. My parents separated when I was a toddler. My Mom and I lived with her parents in the Norwood section of Birmingham – the slum section of that city. When my parents got back together when I was still little more than a toddler, my Dad vowed we were going to live better than that. He moved up to the Chicago area, got work, and then brought us up to join him. For most of my elementary school years, my Dad worked 80 hours a week to make a way for us. It was a time when men and women rarely asked what others could do for them, only that they be allowed to carve a way for themselves through hard work and community. And the determined work of their hands bred real joy and self-worth through overcoming obstacles. I chuckled when I read that Joe's family got their bread each week from the delivery man for Omar Bakeries – a big chain of bakeries in the Midwest. The first job my Dad got when he brought us north was as a delivery driver for Omar Bakeries.

As kids we got the rudimentary tools for forming healthy communities by playing with each other. Often, we had to make up our own rules to make things go smoothly. For four or five years, I put together a sandlot baseball league that had the whole neighborhood participating – and their visiting relatives. Anyone, no matter what age, could play. To facilitate that, our rule was that the little kids on each team would have their hits count for the team, but not their outs. It helped develop the younger players – and kept it fun for all. It became a proud rite of passage when a little kid got good enough that his outs counted as well as his hits. It was through the direct interaction with each other that we all learned how to smooth out the rough edges and make it into a joyful, fun time working together.

Ironically, in those days, it was the whole village that helped protect the children. If an adult saw you doing something you shouldn't and threatened to call your parents if you didn't knock it off, you straightened right up. We knew that all the adults in the neighborhood were not only watching us, but also watching out for us. Oh, we got into mischief, but we had the good sense to understand when we did that it was mischief we were getting into. Joe presents an affectionate, but candid, look at who we were that will bring a rosy glow of nostalgia to all who lived it.

The darker part of Joe's survey of all the institutions and mores of modern times looks at who we are – and why it is all so dystopian. Technology has given us many advantages, but our abuse of it has atomized all sense of community. Joe makes the critical distinction between observational entertainment and active entertainment. All our video games, social media and spectator activities are observational entertainment. In a healthier America, that was an occasional treat – and most of your observational entertainment involved cheering friends and relatives on in their organized sporting activities. The great bulk of our activities were active entertainment. It is not that this was simply better, but that it was vital in helping us learn how to create functioning social systems. We had to learn how to get along with each other, or there was no entertainment, at all.

This made me think of something my son told me a few years ago. Somewhat mournfully, he observed that his generation had tools for communication that were beyond anything my generation could have dreamed of when we were young – but that my generation knew how to talk with each other, which had become a lost art to his. As I learned that teenage boys rarely build up their courage to even ask a girl out, but ask via a text, it hit home how much we have lost. We are frustrated because we try to build a community having tossed away most of the tools in our box. We have thrown out the baby and kept the bathwater.

Even in the face of all we have lost, Joe does not just look at modern culture through dark-colored glasses. He sees and speaks of the advances we have made in some aspects of medicine and technology and how great a blessing these advances could be if we could get back a sense of community.

Like a gifted coach, he sees what we were, what we are, and how we can meld all those characteristics into a true renaissance built on faith, family and freedom. By no means utopian, Joe is cautiously optimistic about how we can forge a healthy culture once more, if we are committed with our whole hearts under God. This book is a concise analysis and plan for renewal. If we heed Coach Brickner's call to action, we will not remain lost in place in America.

TIme to get the team together and start drilling. The coach has put together a great game plan.

Charlie Johnston
Founder of the Corps of Renewal and Charity (CORAC)
Author of the Blog: A Sign of Hope

America: Lost in Place

Introduction

I wrote quite a bit of my first book ("So, you want to be a Coach...") while relaxing on the beach in Salter Path, NC. I find myself here again at the beach contemplating life at 70 plus in a tumultuous world. Being this old, I have lived through some difficult times here in the U.S. The most turbulent would have been the late sixties/early seventies with the civil rights movement and the Viet Nam war going on.

At that time I was finishing up college and facing the lottery for young men drafted into the military. People in the U.S. were generally not happy. Times didn't change much until Ronald Reagan replaced Jimmy Carter in the White House and the economy took off.

> [Shortly after President Richard Nixon had ended the disastrous war in Southeast Asia, President Carter was "held hostage" by the Ayatollahs of Iran who had overthrown the Iranian government. The 144 Americans being held hostage in Iran cast a dark shadow over the everyday news while President Carter was in office. However, shortly after Reagan took over, the hostages were released, Reagan introduced tax cuts, and the economy took off. The American disposition improved significantly rather quickly.]

In 2022 we face even more problems than in the late sixties/early seventies.

- We had been engaged in the longest war in our history in Afghanistan, which ended in what may be called the worst military withdrawal in the history of the United States. We left both Americans and allies behind enemy lines.

- Russia has invaded Ukraine. Our leaders are flirting with nuclear war with Russia by our response to this terrible act and our lack of trying to negotiate a settlement early on.
- A deadly virus gained a chokehold on America. Those in charge of our government are forcing citizens to take an experimental gene-therapy injection, regardless if they are Covid-survivors with antibodies that keep them from contracting or spreading the disease.
- The civil rights gains since the sixties have been ignored by the main news media and a serious racial divide has been re-introduced into our country.
- The citizens of the U.S. are strongly divided between the conservative principles our country was founded on and a more liberal ideology that wants to rid the country of many of those principles in the name of "progress."
- Many are claiming the Supreme Court is illegitimate after the overturning of Roe v. Wade. (Interestingly, all the Supreme Court did was return the authority back to each state to decide the abortion issue, which appears to me to be democracy personified.)
- God has been removed from our schools, place of work, some monuments, and was even attempted to be removed from the platform of the Democrat Party in a recent presidential election.
- Men claim to be women, women to be men, or people can even claim to be neither a man nor a woman.
- You can't speak in public without someone being offended and accusing you of being a racist or some other terrible name.
- Fossil fuels have been demonized. Renewables are claimed to be our only energy hope for the climate's future. Meanwhile, energy prices are the highest ever recorded and inflation has gone through the roof.
- Some people hate the police and have defunded it, while crime has skyrocketed around the country.
- The Federal Government ignores our immigration laws. People celebrate anyone who can sneak across our border and live in our country without going through the proper protocol to be legally in our country.

- Christians are targeted as bigots, while non-Christian religions are looked upon benevolently.
- Half the country is "up in arms" over 19 children being murdered in Uvalde, Texas, understandably, but is strongly supportive of killing 650,000 children in the womb each year.
- Governmental agencies appear to be being used for political purposes. Many conservatives' homes are being raided by the FBI, while liberals breaking the law targeting the homes of Supreme Court Justices with protests, experience no legal repercussions.

I could go on and on – but you get the point. Times are tumultuous and our country is deeply divided.

Being where I am today in my life's continuum, I feel sort of like an editor who is three-fourths of the way through a book and knows the ending, but is still in a position to be able to change subsequent chapters if given the opportunity by the author. Time is such a great teacher, but unfortunately many of us do not take the opportunity to reflect on the past and learn the lessons of others – or sometimes even our own life's lessons.

If you read my first book, you know that I try to be spiritually grounded in the Catholic faith. In my opinion, you can't be Catholic if you don't read and study the Bible. The bible is full of not only life's lessons, but also nations' or peoples' lessons. How many times In the bible have you read about God's Chosen People, the Jews, having things go their way as long as they honored and worshiped God and followed His commands? But the Jews of the bible are just like the Americans of today – they did not know how good they had it until they stopped honoring and worshipping God and following His commands. Over and over you read about the Jews drifting away from their God, only to be conquered by a godless people who took away their freedom and their opportunity to worship their God. And over and over the Jews would realize their mistake, repent, and be restored by God to their former prosperous existence. This cycle is repeated so many times in the bible that when you are reading it you think "How stupid were the Jews? Couldn't they learn from their past?" Well, welcome to America.

In my opinion, we, as a country, are at a fork in the road. We can choose to learn from the past and return to our former ways of living with morals and righteousness. Or, we can follow a "new road" of defining freedom as doing whatever you want, whenever you want, wherever you want. What amazes me is that we are supposedly the most learned people of all time, with knowledge, facts, and historical perspective one click away on our computers. But still, we are wallowing into the mire that brought down great kingdoms like ancient Rome and Greece, Napoleon's France and the Czar's Russia, etc. Why don't we learn from the past? Why do we think we are smarter or wiser than those who came before us? Why do we think we can "have it all" without sacrificing what is necessary to warrant living a great life?

What follows are the recollections of someone who has looked back and put into perspective those things that made our country and its people great, starting with each person as an individual. I compare how things were during America's glory years following World War II and where we are today. I try to impartially evaluate life "back then" compared to life today and point out where things are better and where things are worse. I know you won't agree with some of my recollections and /or opinions – but that is okay. In America, that is what our founding principles stood for – freedom to express oneself without fear of repercussion from the government, but rather having healthy debate with each other.

Also, know that I may say things bluntly and you may be offended. That is not my intention. I am not trying to be mean or malicious. I am simply telling you the way I see it, simply and directly, but also humbly.

Finally, I am not trying to deflate your hope in our people or our country with the things I describe in this book. There are many things going in the wrong direction these days, but if we can return to God and the principles that our country was founded on, we will make a speedy recovery and prosper once again, both materially and spiritually. But it has to start with each of us personally. If each of us can get it right for ourselves, then collectively we will get it right as a people. The key to this happening lies in leadership. Who will lead the charge and restore America to our founding principles? Will you and I be leaders, or at least strong followers? Will you join me and dig deep and make the strong effort to revitalize our neighbors and ourselves? If you and I don't do it, then who will?

Chapter 1 - The Way We Were

I grew up in the 50's in Northwestern Ohio. Dad came from a German family who were farmers, and mom came from an Italian immigrant family who worked at whatever jobs they could find to be able to pay the bills. Mom and dad had 2 sons and 2 daughters, in that order. I was the second son, so I was gifted by the good fortune of not having to be reared in the same strict manner that a first child was reared back then.

Dad was a car salesman and mom had been a factory worker until about the time my first sister was born. After that, mom stayed home with us or worked at odd jobs part time. We owned a home in Lima, Ohio, my first few years of existence. When I was about five, we had to move in with my dad's parents for a few years until our financial situation improved. Grandma and Grandpa had a small farm in rural Delphos, Ohio, which, looking back on it now, was such a blessing for us kids growing up. Learning the hard work and discipline involved in running a small farm was invaluable to me, personally. I was still very young at the time, but I loved going out with grandpa on the tractor, even if it was to throw a load of manure on one of his fields.

Back then living on a small farm meant that you not only worked hard to make your own farm profitable, but you always pitched in to help your neighbors keep their farms afloat. Most farmers in that area had one or two tractors, a disc, a plow, a planter, a manure spreader, a mower and a rake that attached to their tractor. One of the neighbors would normally have purchased a hay baler that was used on many of the neighbors' fields besides his own. Some had a corn picker or a wheat/oats harvester. But all of these implements were expensive, so sharing was very common among the farmers of that day.

My favorite time of the year was after the wheat or oats had been harvested, or the clover cut and raked, for then it was time for the hay baler to be wheeled out. The neighboring farmers would all get together and bale the straw or the hay, going from one farm to the next. Whoever's farm was being worked would be in charge of serving lunch and dinner for the whole group. So the wife of that specific farmer would have a modest lunch for the group, but a huge feast for dinner for everyone. One of my favorite times was sitting on the screened-in porch after dinner with Grandpa and the two neighbor brothers, Ray and Ralph Speiles. They would take turns telling the most interesting and unique stories about things that had happened on their property. Most of the time it involved a fox or a wolf or a raccoon. I was mesmerized by these stories, and they almost always ended in a huge group laugh.

So what are my takeaways from this experience?

1. *Sacrifice and discipline.* In order to be successful, a certain level of sacrifice and discipline is required. Grandpa got up every morning at 5 a.m. to milk the cows. He had no choice – if he did not feel good, he did it anyway. The cows had to be milked regardless of the extenuating circumstances. He had to repeat this task again every evening. There was never a day off. Grandpa never once complained, to my knowledge. He just did what he had to do, day in and day out.
2. *Plan and execute*. In order to be successful you have to plan and execute well. Crops grow according to God's schedule, not man's. You have to be ready to plant when the time is right and harvest when the time is right. You have to fertilize and weed the fields in a timely manner. Each crop raised requires a different process and a different schedule. The land itself had to be considered. You can't raise corn every year in the same field because within a few years all the nutrients will be depleted from that field. So, crop rotation is important. Coordinating all these activities and performing them in a timely manner takes detailed planning, followed by effective execution. One small error in planning or delay in execution could cost you a whole field's crop. When you are a small farmer, you can't afford to have one of your fields fail you.
3. *Prayer and Trust in God.* In order to be successful you have to pray often and trust God. Grandpa had no control over the weather. He could not afford to have an irrigation system on his farm, so if the crops needed watering, only a good rain would suffice. Crops also

need sunshine. If it rains too much, the results are just as bad as if it rains too little. The only input humans have into this formula is prayer. I don't remember grandma or grandpa being overly religious, but they did have faith. We prayed before and after every meal and at night before we went to bed. Sometimes when a tornado was threatening we might say a rosary. Grandma and grandpa attended church every Sunday, and grandpa never worked on Sunday, other than milking the cows, regardless of the crop situation. They simply prayed for good weather and a bountiful harvest, and trusted that God would supply what was necessary.

4. *Give as well as accept help.* In order to be successful you have to share as well as accept help. As I mentioned earlier, the way of life on a small farm was to be neighborly, helping others whenever the need arose and accepting help in your time of need. [For some strange reason, I used to love to help grandpa and the neighbors bale hay. Don't ask me why – it is a hot and dirty job. At the end of the day you are covered with chaff, and before we knew of sun screen, you more than likely had a bad sunburn on your arms and neck. My brother often drove the tractor that pulled the hay baler, and I joined the "men" on the trailer (read here: got in the way) that was towed behind the baler. Each man had a bale hook, and as the bale of hay was exiting the baler, you would hook the bale and pull it onto the trailer. You then passed it back to the "stacker" man, who would then stack the bales five or six bales high. When the trailer was full, you would unhook the full trailer and another man on a separate tractor would take the full trailer back to the barn to load the hay into the barn's hay loft. As you can see, it took a minimum of four or five men in order to do this work, so depending upon neighbors to help was simply a way of life.]

Chapter 2 - Simple Times, Simple Formula

Throughout most of my childhood what were known as "Blue Laws" were enforced in Ohio. Blue Laws said that if you were not an essential service, you were not open for business on Sunday. I only remember one restaurant being open in Delphos on Sundays, and I don't remember if any gas stations were open for business. (This predates being able to pump your own gas.) Sunday was truly a day of rest. Families went to church on Sunday morning, had a big dinner after church, then spent the day with the family relaxing and doing things together as a family. When we lived at Grandpa's farm, Grandma would cook the big dinner after church. Everything we had to eat for dinner was from the farm, except maybe the bread. (They called it dinner back then, not lunch. The evening meal was called supper, not dinner.) The bread came from the "Omar Man," who drove his bakery truck from house to house to sell Omar Bakery's goods. I always loved when grandma would get cinnamon rolls in addition to the bread – this was probably the start of my downward journey of eating too many sweets!

I used to help grandma catch the chickens we were going to eat for dinner by using a straightened out wire cloths hanger with the end bent into a small hook. Grandma would tell me which chicken to go after, and we would chase it until we hooked one of its feet. Once you caught the chicken you would place their neck between two nails on a tree stump, chop off the head, and throw the chicken out into the yard and watch it run around in circles until it died. (This is where the expression "Running around like a chicken with your head cut off" came from.) We'd then dip it in scalding hot water, holding it up by its feet until the feathers were saturated with the hot water. This would allow you to easily pluck the feathers. Grandma would then butcher the chicken and then normally fry everything but the guts and the feet. (Remember, the head was already gone.) All the vegetables came from the garden and the fruit from the orchard. The meal was always delicious, and if there were any "scraps" left over, they went to the dogs or the pigs. I simply don't remember "leftovers."

After we left the farm and rented our own farm house, mom would cook the big Sunday dinner after Mass. We still had fried chicken, mashed potatoes, green beans, corn on the cob, and apple or cherry pie for dessert, but the chicken came from the butcher.

When we lived at Grandma's, TV was not a common mode of entertainment. It had just been introduced to the public, so most people still got their news, weather, dramas and comedies by listening to the radio. Since there wasn't much on the radio on Sundays except for religious music and religious programs, and since there was no store or movie theatre open, most families got together with their siblings' families and played cards. Air conditioning was not available to most people, so huge fans would be placed in open windows to circulate the air from outside in the summer time. My folks normally played canasta, but sometimes they would play pinochle. I never really learned the former, but loved playing pinochle. The adults never let the kids play with them, but that was okay – there were normally four or more kids there who knew how to play pinochle.

If the weather was nice enough to be outside, we'd play softball or horseshoes, or my favorite – kick the can! {Kick the can was a "hide-and-go-seek game" where whoever was "it" had to find all the other players who were hiding. Once he/she saw the player, they would both run to the can. The first one there determined not only the fate of the person seen, but also the players in "jail" who had already been caught. If the one seen could kick the can before the "it" person got there, everyone in jail got freed and could go hide again. The game went on until everyone was caught. The best part of the game, though, was when the "it" person strayed from the can to look for the other players who had not yet been caught. One of the still-hiding players could sneak in and kick the can, thus freeing all the players in jail.}

We used to play that game long into the night, when hiding was much easier than during the day. I always wanted to play when my cousin Jimmy was not "it." Even if he was the last one who had not been caught, you had a better than 50-50 chance he would free you. He was as fast as greased lightning, and even if the "it" person had a shorter distance to the can than Jimmy, Jimmy would almost always beat him/her there and "Kick the Can!"

Sundays were truly a special day each week for most people. Like in the beginning, six days of work was followed by a wonderful day of rest.

So what are my takeaways from this experience?

1. *Cherish a day of rest each week.* We all desperately need a weekly day of rest. In today's typical American home, Sunday religious services have given way to the worship of the great soccer ball (or baseball, or basketball, or softball, etc., or whatever it is that you have signed your kids up to play.) Sometimes both parents attend, but normally it's mom who drives the SUV to most events while dad goes golfing with his buddies. If church is attended, the kids are in uniform so that they are not late for the athletic event, even if that means leaving Mass after Holy Communion. {An exception to this behavior is in some black communities. I don't have any statistics to back this up, but my observation is that some black families attend religious services on Sunday morning and then all either go out to dinner (lunch?) at grandma's or a local restaurant. That is refreshing.}
2. *Be real, and not portray fake fun.* Having fun did not involve cell phones, iPads, or any other electronic gadgets. Grown-ups may have stayed indoors at times to socialize, but kids rarely did. We lived outdoors. We either played traditional games or made up our own games. You ran, laughed, screamed, and sometimes just acted silly having a good time with your cousins or your neighbors. You did not have to send pictures or videos to your friends of you having fun – you were actually <u>with</u> your friends having fun.
3. *Appreciate and embrace your family heritage.* Family traditions and first cousins were dear to you. Grandma's house was the gathering place. A real bond between you and your dad's and/or your mom's siblings' kids was important. Your first cousins sometimes became closer to you than even a brother or sister. Family heritage was important. I don't see that much in today's world. As more and

more young people went to college, more of them did not come home after they graduated. Instead, they interviewed and took a job in their field of expertise in a location that presented the best career opportunities for them. In addition, for those who did not go to college and decided to join the workforce after high school, many were forced into moving away after the local job opportunities dried up. Small towns became practically ghost towns as jobs were relocated to bigger cities. For those jobs that normally would be mainstays in small towns, they also were eliminated. Businesses like Walmart, Lowe's, Home Depot, etc. established a regional presence causing grocery stores, drug stores, clothing stores, hardware stores and the like to close in the smaller towns. With that went the jobs, and the effect it had on family get-togethers was significant. People no longer lived close to their cousins – or even their parents. Now the gatherings occur mainly on July 4 or Thanksgiving or Christmas. Getting to know cousins is just not in the mix anymore for many families. The family heritage has taken a significant hit, and may not be able to recover.

4. *The only important messages on the Lord's Day come from God or your family.* After your day of rest (Sunday), you were mentally, physically and spiritually ready to go back to work or school on Monday morning. Getting away from the job for even just one day made a huge difference in your outlook and attitude. Having enjoyed your faith and your family, and not being pulled into "checking on how things are going at work," refreshed the average person back then. Today, you simply can't get away from the job. You are constantly being bombarded with emails and text messages that have to do with either the job itself or related information that shows up and "dings" you on your cell phone. It has become a disease, in my opinion. People today can't go 10 minutes without checking their phones for messages. What could possibly be more important than your God and your family on your day off? Will the world stop rotating if you ignore those messages until Monday?

Chapter 3 - The Three R's

Schools back in the 50's and 60's were pretty simple in their approach to educating the young. The three R's (Reading, Riting, and Rithmetic) were the foundations for what was taught in elementary and high school. Some kids were fortunate to be able to attend kindergarten when they were 5 or 6, but most of us did not attend school until the first grade. Few children knew much about reading, writing or math prior to attending school. The parents and grandparents were busy at home or on the job and did not have time to spend teaching the "youngins" these things. (Remember, there was no TV, so there was no Sesame street or Electric Company for the kids to watch and learn their letters and numbers.) Parents taught them to pray, do chores, and entertain themselves. Schools started with the mere basics of the alphabet and numbers. You were taught how to spell, write cursive and add, subtract, multiply and divide. There were no fancy help aids other than "flash cards," and memorizing was how you learned. I still remember sitting in my second grade class and hoping the nun teaching us would not call on me to recite the alphabet. I was so scared that I would not know it, and dreaded being embarrassed in front of my classmates. (I fortunately made it through it when she actually did call on me – what a confidence builder that was!)

We progressed from grade to grade learning more and more about the three R's, plus music, science, history, geography, religion and proper behavior. (The nuns made sure of that.) In high school these areas were expanded to include biology, chemistry, advanced math, and languages. For those who wanted to go to college, a special "honors" curriculum was offered. For those who did not want to go to college, they still had to do well in all of the basic courses. However, they were also offered vocational courses like shop (home repairs and craftsmanship, including how to use power tools like saws and drills), home economics (sewing, cooking, budgeting), business skills (shorthand, typing, office machines, basic accounting), etc. I was personally taking the college prep track, which was great. The unfortunate part of the college prep track for me was that there were a couple of courses that really did me little good going forward. Biology was okay, but Chemistry and Physics were courses that I took, and did okay in, but didn't retain the information or use it in any beneficial way that I am aware of. I would have loved to have taken shop instead of those couple of courses. I could have learned how to become skilled in woodworking and things like that, or maybe even taken advanced music or art classes.

At our high school, most students' schedules allowed one study hall period a day. I usually completed my math homework during that 40-50 minute period, but in no way was able to get any other subjects' homework assignments completed. What that meant was that when I got home from school (or basketball/baseball practice), I faced at least two hours or more of homework, on average. Similar to grade school, we were assigned homework in every subject every night. Not doing your homework was not an option. Mom would ensure that we completed it every night. The first thing that each teacher did at the beginning of the following day's class was to go around the room and collect your homework. Every assignment was then graded and handed back to you the following day. Homework was a significant part of your grade for each respective class, and a significant part of the learning process.

When my sons were going through grade school and high school in the 70's and 80's, their experience was similar to mine. I don't believe it is that way any longer. Maybe at the private schools students are required to do extensive work out of class time, but I don't believe it is that way at most public schools. In addition, all assignments had to be done by hand – so we were using cursive to complete written assignments and pencils and brains to do mathematical problems. (Many teachers also graded you on "penmanship," insuring you were careful and neat when documenting your assignments.) Today, almost all assignments are done on a computer. Doing a math problem in your head is non-existent. Today students don't even use a calculator to do math – they can use a spreadsheet with formulas that will do the work for them. Researching a subject by getting resource books from the library has given way to simply "Googling it" on your phone or laptop.

Using your brain is now geared to finding the right "app" that will accomplish the task rather than doing the task yourself.

Don't misunderstand me – modern technology is wonderful when used appropriately. Being able to create a formula in a spreadsheet that automatically calculates a complex result is wonderful. But coming up with the formula takes basic and sometimes extensive knowledge in math. If you do not possess that knowledge, you can't create the formula, and technology is of no value to you.

I'd be remiss if I didn't mention the content of the curriculum today compared to earlier years. All along we adults thought that the basics were continuing to be taught in grade schools and high schools around the country. That is, until the pandemic hit. Children of elementary and high school ages were forced to stay home and attend school over the internet, usually via Zoom classes. It was during this time that parents, for the first time, were being exposed to what was actually being taught in the classroom. They were shocked to know that their kids were being exposed to Critical Race Theory (CRT), Gender Identity options, and sex education.

Children of all ages are being "propagandized" into believing that if they are white, they are inherently prejudiced against blacks and other minorities. Plus, because they are white, they are "privileged." Blacks are being taught that they are "victims" and are owed reparation for their great, great, great grandparents being slaves. Included are lessons on how racial prejudice has been built into all of our businesses and institutions. They call it "systemic racism."

Personally, I became aware of some of this by accident after working out one day at the local Community Center. On my way out, I stopped by the county library's "free book" table in the lobby. The books were meant for children and young parents, but I was curious, so I started browsing. I couldn't believe some of the books that the local library was giving away to young readers. The one whose cover struck me most, and the one I picked up and took home, was called "My Anti-Racist Baby." Paging through it raised some concerns. To its credit, it started out by saying that "babies are taught to be racist or anti-racist." But they also say there is no neutrality and that "If you claim to be color-blind, you deny what's right in front of you." It led the reader (or little listener) to believe that children were to make society transform and that they are to make "equity" a reality. I guess the problem I have with this type of literature is that language makes a difference – it propagandizes readers into buying into racism being violent and that people have racist ideas that are hidden. Yes, some people are this way, but most are not. I guess my biggest issue with the book is that it teaches that people are not born anti-racist. I truly believe that when God creates us, we have a conscience that as we mature knows right from wrong. Our conscience knows that racism is wrong. I agree that we have to be taught to be a racist, as the book states. The book actually makes some other good points, but assuming that babies are not anti-racist when they are born just rubs me wrong. Racism is a learned behavior, and anti-racism is innate.

In addition, children were/are being taught that the gender God gave them is not necessarily the correct gender. (Excuse me – teachers would never use the terminology "God gave them." Instead, they would say the gender with which a person was born. As the young ones say, My Bad.) Kids are being taught that they can choose their own gender, or not even have a gender at all! They are being told they can choose to be a boy, even if they were born with female genitalia – and vice versa. They are being taught that others should be forced to call them by their "preferred pronouns," whatever the hell that means. Simultaneously, the kids were being taught sex education even as young as the first and second grade.

Parents were stunned when they discovered what was being taught in the classroom and stormed the local school board meetings in protest, and rightfully so. CRT and gender identity options are both absolute nonsense. Racism is not inherent; it is learned. Privilege is not white. Each of us is in some way privileged. (Good looking people, regardless of gender or color, are privileged. So are those with athletic ability, musical talent, high IQs, good physiques, etc.) It is how you use that privilege that will make a difference in your life, and hopefully the lives of others. Will you use it for good or evil? You won't see that concept being taught in public schools.

As far as gender identity is concerned, I will let you in on a little secret – we don't have a choice. What we were born with is what we get. I can't become a woman by simply saying I feel like I am a woman. I can say it all day long, but it won't change anything. I was born a man, and unless I have some radical surgery replacing my genitalia to some fake man-made genitalia, I remain a man. Pushing this gender identity garbage, especially on confused and impressionable teenagers (and younger), will ruin many lives.

Concerning sex education for our children provided in the classroom, there is no place for it. Sex education is extremely personal. It is a parental responsibility and right. Only a parent knows when the time is right for a child to be taught about sex, love, and permanent commitments. Only a parent knows how to appropriately approach the subject, and how to lovingly communicate with their child from a human and spiritual perspective.

What is sad is that people in general, businesses and governmental bodies are not standing up and saying that these educational initiatives are wrong. In actuality, many are going along with it so that they are not singled out and punished for going against these fringe initiatives. You see it in TV and print ads, corporate human resources organizations, local schools districts and the like. When is someone going to have the guts to stand up and say "This is BS and I am not going to stand for it any longer?" Instead, employees are forced to attend CRT and "equity" training conducted by the HR department. You have educators and governmental officials letting everyone know what their personal pronouns are. You have professors actually losing their jobs or quitting because they refuse to go along with this nonsense. (e.g., Dr. Jordan Peterson)

When are we, as a nation, going to declare "Enough is enough?" When are we going to stop this woke babble and start using some good old common sense? It is time. If not us, then who?

So what are my takeaways from this experience?

1. *Learn the basics and create the foundation for future success*
2. *Use the learned basics to become self-reliant*
3. *Stay relevant, but also stay grounded*
4. *Monitor everything that is being taught to our children, ensuring that it is based on facts, not ideology*

Chapter 4 - Advanced Education

I was blessed to be the first person on either side of my family to go to a four-year college. Back in those days most young people followed in their parents' footsteps and most parents I knew did not go to college. On the farm it was pretty much assured that the boys would help dad farm and eventually take over the farm when dad passed on. The daughters usually married a neighbor farm boy at a relatively young age and became a farmer's wife with all its duties and responsibilities. Non-farm kids' parents more often than not had labor intensive jobs and the boys normally got those same types of jobs after getting out of high school. Some kids had a parent who had a professional job that required an advanced degree such as a doctor, lawyer, accountant, teacher, etc. These were the kids who usually went to college, but they were in the minority. Quite often, even if a person wanted to go to college, they were prevented from doing so due to the cost. I would have fallen into that category if I had not received a scholarship to play basketball in college.

Because of the smaller numbers of high school students who pursued a college degree, high schools, as I mentioned in an earlier chapter, offered a "shop" or "home-ec" track that taught them practical skills. They could use these skills to gain employment after high school. These classes might include woodworking, automotive repair, welding, etc. People in our town who got a good paying job out of high school at the local factory were looked on favorably, even more so sometimes than a person who received a college scholarship.

Things have changed drastically in today's world. It is practically expected that everyone go to college to get a good job. That is so wrong in my opinion. We need good plumbers, electricians, carpenters, mechanics, repairmen, truck drivers, etc. Now, more than ever, if someone has an aptitude and desire for these types of jobs, why discourage them? Why try to make them believe they have to go to college to be successful? Why not encourage them to pursue these jobs and pave the way for them by offering training in these fields in high school? Years of pushing kids to go to college have created a catastrophic student loan debt crisis in America, and many of these debtors can't find good employment.

It is probably true that in the "old days" there were some who became farmers or laborers who could have become good engineers or physicians. But I believe we have now erred on the other side - we are pushing young people who would excel at practical careers into a college track that leads nowhere.

So what is the solution? I've mentioned part of it above. Education. We need to offer practical classes at the high school level (including budgeting, marriage relationship prep, and raising a family in addition to "shop.") We also need to incorporate a mentorship or apprenticeship program at the high school level. This would include "shadow days" where students can shadow a person for a couple of days who actually performs the job or jobs that the student might be interested in. Shadowing before actually taking it in class or being mentored or becoming an apprentice would increase the success rate of such a program. And lastly, working with local businesses to set up internships and job placement services would seal the deal. Individuals would win as well as local businesses would win.

Now let's move on to college education. I taught MBA courses for over 17 years. I loved teaching the Executive Master of Business Administration (EMBA) courses, where students were required to have five or more years of business management experience plus a college degree in order to be accepted into the program. These students not only forced you to "know your stuff," they also challenged you to keep current with business trends and nuances. They were highly motivated to learn, not to "get a grade." I did not find those same qualities when teaching MBA courses to recent grads. The mindset with these students was equivalent to their mindset as undergrads – what does it take to get a "B?" Because of this attitude of studying for a grade instead of for knowledge, I also discovered that what they were supposed to have learned in previous classes was not retained. They would take a course, get their A or B, and then pull a Hillary Clinton and wipe their memory clean. I wasn't the only one to experience this. My faculty colleagues confirmed my observation.

My solution to this conundrum was to incorporate business simulations into my courses. The student not only had to learn the topic or technique, they also had to demonstrate how to successfully use it in the simulation. Grades were based on simulation results, not on a written test on the topic. I realize not all courses can do this, but many can. For those that can't, using a little ingenuity might produce the same result. Keep in mind that the goal is to require the student to successfully demonstrate the use of the technique, concept, principle, etc. being taught. For example, when I taught international finance to the undergraduate classes, I taught the principles of foreign exchange, monetary policy, etc. However, I also taught "rule of law," government stability, infrastructure, etc. The students learned these concepts just fine, but rather than test them on this knowledge, instead I created a scenario whereby they had to build a fictitious plant that produced a product that they had to export. They also had to import a specific product. I broke the class up into five teams, each team representing a specific geographical region as defined by the World Bank. Within each team/region, each student had to choose a country that they would represent. During the semester each principle that was taught had a graded homework assignment turned in by the team and a separate report by the student. The team reported regional data and the student reported country data.

For the final exam, each team had to turn in a detailed document and make a formal presentation concerning the scenario mentioned above. They had to choose which country in their region that would be used to build the factory and just how they would export its product and to whom in that market. They also had to provide a detailed plan on how they were going to import a specific product and market it locally in each country in their region.

The presentation was made in front of the entire class and invited faculty members. Part of their grade was determined by me based upon how convincing this presentation was compared to the other regions' presentations, and what facts they used to justify their plans. In addition each team graded the other teams' presentations for accuracy, credibility and reasoning.

By teaching the course in this manner, I forced the students to use what they learned. It obviously took a lot more work for me (and the students) in designing and grading the course. But they walked away really understanding international finance as well as international marketing. In my opinion that is how college courses should be taught.

[I might also mention that I recently participated in a podcast that hosted a professor who, along with his professor wife, is starting a new, unique college concept. To be located in New Mexico, this college's curriculum will contain not only the liberal arts, but also the practical arts. It will be somewhat like the curriculum I described earlier for "shop" in high school. Included will be courses on carpentry, etc., as well as internships and apprenticeships at local businesses. Start-up date for the new college is the fall of 2023 or 2024. I will be extremely interested in following its progress.]

Finally, it is no secret that our colleges and universities are staffed by liberal instructors and administrators. I read somewhere recently that over 90% of college professors vote the Democrat ticket, which has turned uber-liberal. For decades they have allowed their political ideology to infiltrate their classes. Here is what I believe: college educators should keep politics and ideology out of the classroom, unless you are teaching a course in Political Science. Being a professor, you have a huge influence on framing the minds of your students. Your job is not to get them to lean left or right. Your job is to make them think clearly and make informed choices. Too many of today's colleges and universities propagandize our young people instead of teaching them to think critically. We don't need robots in our country. We need people who use common sense and gain knowledge and make decisions based on facts. They need real life experiences to help them to make decisions for themselves, their families, their communities, and their country. If we can develop that kind of citizenry, we will continue to be world leaders on all fronts.

So what are my takeaways from this experience?

1. *<u>Teach the fundamentals</u> at all levels in our schools which will <u>allow the students to make informed practical decisions</u> in all phases of their lives.*
2. *Being able to learn to <u>critically think</u> should be the goal of college instruction.*

Chapter 5 - Jobs and Careers

Looking back and comparing the past to today, jobs and careers are areas that have seen significant change. Where and when I grew up, once you had a job you stayed in that job until you retired, got laid off, or got fired. People really appreciated having a good paying, steady job. Many in our community worked in factories, which usually were the best paying jobs. Back then Lima Steel, Lima Locomotive, Westinghouse, Standard Oil and Ford, among others, were the economic backbone of our city and country. If you had a job at one of those places, you and your family were very appreciative - even if you had to work second or third "trick" (shift).

Automation hit manufacturing in those days, but technology and sophisticated robotics were still in the future. My mother worked second trick (3:30 PM to 11:30 PM) and she wound jet motors (whatever that means) at Westinghouse. She was happy to have a job but always feared being laid off, like many others. The only way she and others would consider changing jobs would be if she actually did get laid off. These certainly weren't glamorous jobs, but they were considered good jobs and employees would often try to get their relatives a job at the same place where they worked.

I don't remember hearing the word "career" until I started interviewing for jobs as a senior in college. In those days, once you started working for a company, you normally stayed at that company until you retired. The concept of a career was used internally more so than externally. My colleagues and I had often talked about our management careers. However, we were always referring to our progress up the ladder in our own company, which was Southwestern Bell Telephone Company at the time.

My, how things have changed. Today it is highly unusual for someone to spend their entire working career with the same company. People change jobs often, using job change as a method of improving a person's career. One of my sons has worked for at least eight to 10 companies over his 30 year career, and every time he changed jobs, he got a better deal. That is somewhat typical today, I believe. (Although, I accused him of being the best "Interviewee" of all time.)

Jobs themselves have changed significantly also. Technology has touched practically every industry. Recall any job from 20 years ago and think about it today - if the job still even exists. We used to have folks who came by monthly or bimonthly to read our water meter and electricity meter. No longer. A computer keeps a real time record of our usage today. Remember taking your car to a mechanic to see if he could determine what was causing engine problems? No longer. The mechanic hooks your car up to a computer and the computer runs diagnostics to determine the problem and its causes. Everything is like that today. If you are not computer literate, your job selection is severely reduced.

I believe things are better today than they used to be from a job perspective, but maybe not so much from a career perspective. There are many mundane as well as unhealthy or dangerous jobs that are handled today by computers and/or robots. I don't believe that jobs are as physical as they used to be, but I do believe they are more stressful. I'm not sure if today's jobs are more rewarding, but they probably are, because the employee is likely to be involved in multiple tasks rather than a single task. So my take is that we are better off today compared to jobs in the good old days.

I don't quite feel the same about careers. As I had mentioned earlier, in the past a career for most industries was more internal than "external." You had a career "within" a company, not by moving from company to company. There was an unwritten "loyalty" commitment between the employee and the employer - and it went both ways. The employees seldom sought out jobs at other companies, and employers looked at employees as part of the family. Companies did not look for ways to eliminate employees with buyouts or early retirement plans. They actually celebrated an employee's longevity of service. When I worked for Bell, we rewarded employees for each five years of service they achieved. Depending upon the length of service achieved, a nice gift was presented to the celebrant of a party on the company's dime and time. For my 25th service anniversary, tons of people attended from all over our five-state region. And if you thought service anniversaries were a big deal, you should have seen the retirement parties!

Retirees were special people to most companies. They were welcomed with open arms whenever they showed up back at the work location after retiring. (At Bell, one of my responsibilities when I became a third level manager was to contact a list of retired third-level and above employees at least annually. I was to make sure they were doing OK, and help resolve any problems they may be encountering with health, benefits, finances, etc. They were still part of the Bell family.)

Many mid-level and above managers became "mentors." Community service was something you were graded on on your annual appraisal. Giving 1% of your salary to United Way was mandatory for managers. All of these things went into your "career development."

Today there's nothing close to a loyalty bond between employer and employee. Employers try to find every way possible to reduce employees (labor expense) and reduce benefits. Most companies don't really care about their employees other than how efficiently they perform their jobs. Employees, on the other hand, have no sense of loyalty to the company and will jump to another company the first time a better offer comes along. Careers, therefore, have to be seen as "dog eat dog." The environment that used to exist between companies in the same industry now exists within companies. Mentors may still exist, but it is from a bottom up perspective, not a top down. A mentor is now someone who can help you get ahead, not necessarily develop/groom you for a more responsible position. The dog eat dog attitude has made internal careers more difficult. Plus, with no company loyalty, why not seek career opportunities externally? I'm sure you know many people who have changed jobs (i.e., companies) five, six, eight or ten times throughout their working life.

Today's environment has created more of a "transaction" commitment versus a "loyalty" commitment, according to Bill Toepfer, a former nation-wide Mortgage Company CEO. He saw companies paying for skill sets, and, in turn, employees honing skill sets to make themselves more attractive. Toepfer says that companies value knowledge and expertise while employees pursue opportunities whereby they can increase their knowledge and expertise. In so doing, employees make themselves more valuable. The transaction then is that the employee brings knowledge and expertise to the table and the company pays for this value. At any time, the transaction can be terminated by either party. The company can indicate that the knowledge and expertise is no longer needed or of value to them. The employee can move on if they find another company who values their knowledge and expertise more than their present employer does. Since this understanding is shared, all seems fair to both parties today.

So what are my takeaways from this experience?

1. Jobs are probably _more interesting and technically challenging_ than they used to be.
2. Careers are much _more difficult and may be less rewarding_ today than in the past.
3. Loyalty between employer and employee is rare. Everyone now has to _look out for themselves_ and put themselves ahead of the company, because most companies put the _bottom line ahead_ of their employees.
4. _Knowledge and expertise are of value_ to an employer, while knowledge and expertise are what is for sale by an employee.

Chapter 6 – Money

I was at the beginning (1948) of the baby boomer generation (1946 – 1964), so I have been blessed to witness all the changes that have occurred since the end of World War II. There have been many good changes, and many that have been not-so-good. Money is one that has been both good and bad, in my opinion.

Growing up we were rather poor, so money was something that was always a variable in every decision made by my family. We lived pretty much from paycheck to paycheck. My family appreciated the value of a dollar, and we kids appreciated the few luxuries that we had growing up. (A new bike, new school clothes, etc.) We never went on vacation, and if dad had not been a car salesman, we would never have even seen the inside of a new car. We didn't buy things we couldn't afford. Back then, credit was rare. You might have a credit account at the local corner grocery store, but in almost all cases, other than for a house mortgage, you paid cash for your purchases. This effectively limited what you purchased and when you purchased it. Some stores had "lay-away" accounts where you would put something back that you wanted to buy and then pay a small portion on the balance each week or month until you had paid for the item. At that point, you could pick up the item from "lay-away." Basically, if you wanted something, you saved your money until you had enough to buy the item. I think that was a good thing.

In 1950 the first universal credit card was introduced to the U.S. It was called the Diner's Club card. (I never knew anyone who had a Diner's Club card.) Then in 1958, American Express brought out their credit card. It wasn't until around 1966 that bank credit cards were introduced to many states, with the forerunner of VISA being the first one. This changed America. In the late sixties, people started buying things without first saving their money to pay for it. Purchasing habits changed, as did attitudes towards materialism, in my opinion. Now if you wanted something, you "charged" it. The hidden consequence behind these purchases went beyond people being able to afford the purchase – they now were paying much more for that item because they could not pay off their credit card bill each month. They had to pay high interest rates on their balance due for these purchases, so, over time, the item may cost twice or even more than twice its original price. This eventually robbed the purchaser of being able to buy other needed items and caused many people to get into deep financial trouble with large amounts of credit card debt. Again, as we will find in many other topics in this book, lack of self-discipline has had catastrophic consequences.

Another factor that affected money was when we got off the gold standard. In 1900, President William McKinley signed the Gold Standard Act, which established gold as the sole basis for redeeming paper currency. The U.S. was on the gold standard most of the following years - although the U.S. and Europe suspended it in 1913 so that they could print dollars to pay for the war effort. Being on the gold standard limited the amount of money that could be printed by tying paper money to a specific value in gold. The U.S. had to have enough gold to back up its currency, so they were limited to how much money they could print and introduce into the economic system. (It also discouraged government budget deficits and debt, which couldn't exceed the supply of gold.) In August of 1971, Richard Nixon, who was President at the time, tied the dollar to a specific value of gold ($38/ounce). By 1976 the value of the dollar was officially decoupled from gold, ending the gold standard. By getting off the gold standard, the U.S. could print money without being held accountable to a related value of something of worth (like gold, silver, diamonds, etc.). Not being held in check, dollars could flood the system and allow the expansion of our economy. The downside was that it also spurred inflation and debt.

There are numerous arguments as to the pros and cons of the gold standard. I won't get into the weeds on these arguments. But what I will point out is that when you are on some sort of value-related asset backed standard, you are limited in spending (printing money) by the total value of those assets. When you decouple your currency from the value of these assets, you are now only limited by your appetite for monetary growth. Today our federal government is not limited by any asset backed value. It can print, and has been printing, money like it grows on trees. Through sophisticated artificial mechanisms, our government has been able to artificially limit inflation. (e.g., expanding the balance sheet by buying government bonds on the open market, known as "quantitative easing.") That is finally coming to an end. You see inflation raising its ugly head everywhere these days (highest in over 40 years), and our federal leaders have no self-discipline to stop this self-destruction. They continue to pass bill after bill that spends money without having the tax revenue to pay for this spending spree. Again, lack of self-discipline is moving us dangerously close to economic disaster.

So what are my takeaways from this experience?

1. *Discipline is a winner*. The lack of the discipline which existed "in the old days," has caused Americans individually and the U.S. collectively to go into enormous debt. For those people who were personally disciplined from a financial perspective, they can weather the storm for a while. However, due to runaway inflation, they too will suffer the loss of their current standard of living. Things are going to get bad, and probably quickly.
2. *Own hard assets.* The only hedge against being wiped out would be to own hard assets, which is not so easy to do. Gold and precious metals are expensive, and some, like silver, are too bulky to be able to easily store in a safe place that only you have knowledge of and access to these materials. Land is a good option if you can find some that is not being gobbled up by the wealthy, corporations, or foreign governments. Some people recommend bitcoin and similar vehicles, but they are not backed by any assets at all! It is a real challenge to provide a safe financial back-up plan today. The days of retiring and living a "good life" until the Creator calls you are more than likely over, at least until sound monetary policy is reintroduced.

Chapter 7 – Shopping

I hate to shop (unless it is at Dollar Tree). It is not that I am cheap, I just don't like shopping. Like most men, when I shop I have one or two things at the most in mind. I want to go directly to the item I am considering purchasing and make the decision to buy it or not. (Normally, I have already made the decision to buy it or else I would not be in the store.) I will admit that I will look for bargains on that specific item, but if I need or want it, price usually isn't a big factor. My wife realized my dislike for shopping shortly after we were married, so she does not bug me to go "shopping" with her, except twice a year when Dillard's used to have its ridiculous sales and discounted their clothes by like 75%. I kind of enjoyed going with her on those trips – not that I need anything clothes-wise, but rather for the challenge of finding something that is really nice for practically nothing. Now that is a fun game.

Shopping when I grew up was an occasional outing for our family. As I had mentioned earlier, we didn't have much money. So, our shopping was usually for school clothes and supplies in August and possibly for Christmas gifts in November/December. We would frequent the locally owned small businesses most of the time, although that pattern changed in the 60's when "Shopping Malls" became popular. Regional shopping centers were normally located on the outskirts of bigger towns and drew people from as far as 25 to 50 miles away. They were convenient because they always had huge parking lots that were free. (Parking downtown to shop included worrying about, first, finding a spot to park, and then worrying about the parking meter running out before you got back to the car.) Malls also normally contained two large anchor stores, one at each end of the mall. Quite often J.C. Penney would be one anchor and Sears would be the other. In between the anchor stores would be many smaller retail stores selling practically anything you needed. These malls, in many cases, made the downtown retail stores disappear in the larger towns and smaller cities, turning "downtown" into "ghost-town." It was kind of sad to watch this happen because towns' downtowns had been so vibrant, and then they were desolate.

If you did not want to physically go shopping, your only alternative was to buy things out of a store's catalog. The big stores would create huge colored catalogs and mail them to peoples' homes. If you wanted to buy something from the catalog, you would look it up and determine what size, color, etc. that you wanted, and then fill out a form that was included as part of the catalog. I am not sure exactly how you paid for it before the credit card industry became viable. I believe you wrote a check for the cost of the item plus the shipping and handling to mail it to you. My guess is that the companies, after receiving your check and order form, would wait 7 days or so before filling the order to make sure your check cleared. So, usually about two to three weeks after ordering an item, you received it in the mail. I guess catalogs were the forerunners of Amazon.

Advertising was done by putting sales ads in the local newspaper or sending a flyer via mail to your home. Radio ads were also used extensively, and later when TVs became ubiquitous, TV advertising was also used. Radio and TV ads were much more expensive than paper ads, so smaller businesses commonly stuck to print media for their advertising.

Another promotional tool used back then was trading stamps, most notably the "S&H green stamp." When you purchased things in certain grocery stores, department stores or gas stations, the store would give you a number of stamps based on the total amount of money you spent. They also provided you with a book into which you glued the stamps by licking the back of each stamp. When you filled up a book, you could redeem it for merchandise provided by S&H's (Sperry & Hutchinson company) catalog. Almost all shoppers saved green stamps. It was a way to get something "for nothing" that you probably wouldn't have been able to afford. (Top Value stamps were another type of stamp that was also offered to shoppers.)

We were like most of our neighbors – we normally wouldn't buy anything until it went on sale. That was okay with me – as long as I had a ball (whatever season it was at the time), I was happy.

The telephone was not used for selling. You used the telephone to talk briefly with family, friends and neighbors, since almost all phones were on "party lines." A party line was where from four to eight homes were all on the same line. In grandma's home, where she had a fancy new rotary dial phone, before trying to dial a number you had to lift the receiver and listen to make sure someone wasn't on the line talking to someone else. If someone was on the line, you hung up and tried later. (Except for Thelma, who would stay on the line and listen in.) When we moved to a rental farm a few miles from grandma, we had an old crank phone. Our telephone number was one long and one short. It, also, was a party line. The big difference was that on our crank phone party line, the phone rang regardless of whose phone on the party line was trying to be reached. You had to listen carefully to make sure you didn't pick up when someone called one short and one long or two longs. The downside of this system whereby all phones on the party line rang whenever there was a call coming in was twofold:

1. Your phone would be an annoyance due to its ringing all the time and it wasn't for you
2. The difficulty of distinguishing between a long and a short! Depending upon the caller, every person had a different interpretation of what a long was versus a short.

(Oh, another downside was that Louise, Thelma's sister, now picked up the phone to listen in on every call that was made.) The upside to the system was that calls were purposeful – you did not get solicitation calls. Advertising/selling had not reached this technology yet.

[This has more to do with telephone use than selling, but I do recall how awkward it was to use the phone for a personal call back when I was young. There was only one phone in the house, and whoever was on the phone could be heard by everyone. Being young and shy (as opposed to old and shy as I am now), trying to "sell" my value as a good date to a cute gal from school was hard enough without having your big brother and little sister eavesdropping. The only salvation was if you were fortunate enough to have a very long cord on your phone, you might be able to stretch it all the way to the hall closet and shut the door behind you.]

As you certainly realize, shopping has changed drastically over time. There are still some stores located in downtown areas of towns and cities, and there are still some regional shopping malls around. But Walmart has now replicated what shopping malls did in their early days – they have practically wiped out small town stores. Retail stores in small towns simply can't compete price-wise or selection-wise with Walmart, whose strategy was to build regional stores just outside the city limits of a town. Walmart stores carried clothes, shoes, household items, etc., so you saw clothing & shoe stores as well as furniture stores in town close. Then Walmart introduced groceries and pharmacies to their inventory, and you saw the local grocery stores and pharmacies close. Not too long after this Lowe's or Home Depot would put in a regional store, and the hardware stores and lumber yards would close in town. Now many small towns' downtowns are boarded up, thanks to the big box stores.

There are still a few industries that use catalogs mailed to the home as a way of generating sales, but you can probably count them on one hand. The internet has replaced the catalog. Practically every business now has an online presence. You can simply "Google" the company name and click on their website and you will gain access to their whole inventory. A few clicks of items on the screen will put those items in a "shopping cart" for you. You then enter in your payment method (credit/debit card, PayPal, or a similar payment service, etc.) and within days you will receive the item you ordered. The king of all websites for ordering practically anything is Amazon. They more than dominate online purchases. Shopping now, from the comfort of your home (or from the comfort of your computer attached to your hand) is simple, pretty safe, and easy. Online shopping has made "brick and mortar" stores unnecessary, and this has changed drastically how people shop.

Shopping today, at least from a man's perspective, is so much better than it was when I was growing up. If you are a person who shops for the purpose of enjoyment, you will probably disagree with the previous statement. It is hard to find a row of stores where you can pop in and see what's for sale unless you can find an existing shopping center or a unique area of town that hosts boutique or antique shops. For the social shopper, things are not so good anymore. However, for the shopper who wants to find items, purchase them, and get them quickly and conveniently, today's shopping experience is a great improvement over the "old days."

So what are my takeaways from this experience?

1. *Technology has driven both good and bad outcomes for shoppers/citizens.* The mode of shopping has changed drastically due to technology and to the development of big box stores. From strictly a convenience perspective, this has been a good change. From a social perspective and a community involvement perspective, this has been disastrous. Many small towns have become ghost towns due to these two factors.

Chapter 8 - Entertainment

My, my - how things have changed in the field of entertainment. Technology is the main driver behind the huge changes I have witnessed over the years, but content has also changed drastically.

Let me start with the content side of it and weave in the technology influence. Back in the day (50's and early 60's), the main source of information and entertainment was the radio. There weren't any good FM stations in those years – AM was all that people could listen to in almost all locations in the US. I vividly remember sitting in Grandma's kitchen next to the radio and listening to "The Lone Ranger" on certain evenings each week, or Amos 'n' Andy or The Jack Benny Show. You could also listen to music, but your choices were limited – pop, country & western, and sometimes the blues.

Daytime radio had news shows – my favorite was "Paul Harvey." He used to be on for about 30 minutes around noon each day with the latest news from around the country. His news, however, was not what you hear today with this murder and that scandal, etc. He was a story-teller, and his newscasts were extremely entertaining. His content was based on facts, and his stories ranged from unique animal scenarios to interesting personal tales about famous and infamous people. His trademark was telling you an anecdote about someone or something that kept you in the dark as to who or what it was. At the very end of his program, he would have a short commercial and come back with "the rest of the story." It was during this brief period when he would let you in on the secret, and then he would say, "And now you know...the rest of the story!" Immediately he would then sign off by saying "This is Paul Harvey...Good Day" with a cheery rise in his voice when he said "Day." I am not sure about city folks, but rural people listened to Paul Harvey every day. He was kind of like a folksy Walter Cronkite – you could trust that what he reported was true.

By the mid-fifties television sets became affordable and many homes added a TV set to the living room. They were all black and white programs back then, and many of the radio shows converted to the new media once people started buying TVs. My favorites, being a kid, were westerns, especially the Lone Ranger, Roy Rogers & Dale Evans, Gene Autry, and Sky King (a more modern day rancher who had an airplane that was involved every week in solving a crime). Sunday night you watched Bishop Fulton J. Sheen and became a little more holy or the Ed Sullivan Show and actually saw people who you had listened to on the radio for years without knowing what they looked like! There were a few variety shows like Ed Sullivan and some comedies like Jack Benny, but for some reason westerns were the people's choice. Cheyenne, Sugarfoot, Paladin (Have Gun, Will Travel), Gunsmoke – I could go on and on naming westerns that were popular evening programs. Again, all these programs were in black & white. My dad, however, had an ingenious idea of how to make them color. He bought a piece of plastic that fit over the front screen of the TV. The plastic piece was broken into 3 different colored sections – the top was light blue, the middle was light amber, and bottom was green. Viola! We had color TV!!

Record players back then played 78RPM (revolutions per minute) records, but two new sizes were introduced in the 50's. LPs (Long Play) records were 33 1/3 rpms and held multiple songs (albums), and 45 rpm records were smaller and held just one song on each side of the disk, similar to the old 78s. The 45s were the ones that were used in the ever popular "juke boxes" you found in the local hamburger shop. I don't remember ever owning a 78rpm record – most of that music was 1940's vintage and was from the "big band" era. I hated that music. My records were mostly 45s, especially after Elvis Presley, Johnny Cash, and Jerry Lee Lewis hit the scene in the mid-50's. Once Rock 'n Roll took over the airwaves, kids started buying 45s by the droves. A huge boost to the music industry was provided when the transistor radio was introduced in the 50's. Now you could actually carry a radio with you and listen to music – you did not have to be in a building or a car. The transistor radio changed the industry.

Movie theatres were popular then. Going to a Saturday Matinee was pretty cool, and the adults would go to the Friday or Saturday night movie as part of a date night. Drive-in movies were also very popular, but not so much with parents of young daughters! Some movies made their way on to TV, but most people still took in their movies on the "big screen."

Entertainment was simple. Your choices were limited by technology, unlike today. Content was also very simple. There were dramas, comedies, variety shows, and westerns on TV. All had to meet strict censorship guidelines. You didn't hear cursing or witness steamy sex scenes – those were left to the imagination. A parent did not have to worry about what was being shown or said if their children were watching TV or listening to the radio. America and Americans were decent. Looking back, that is such a refreshing thought.

Sports also provided entertainment back then, but not anything like today. From a national standpoint, there was the Saturday Baseball "Game of the Week" with Dizzy Dean and Pee Wee Reese. That's it – one game each week on Saturday afternoon. If you wanted to see a normal major league baseball game you drove to the stadium and watched a game. Tickets and parking were reasonably priced, but food and drinks were a little expensive. However, it was a real treat to go to a live game, and you would tell all your friends for weeks on end about the game and your favorite players. (For me it was Rocky Colavito and the Cleveland Indians.) Football was similar – there was a Saturday college game of the week and the NFL would at least show the local team on area TV stations on Sunday afternoon. The NBA was seldom on TV – even the playoffs. Every so often they would have Bill Russell and the Celtics playing on TV against whomever Wilt Chamberlain was playing for at the time. But these were the exception.

I guess it would be fair to say that pro sports back then were not such a big deal. Sports entertainment centered around local high schools. Back in the 50's and 60's school consolidation had not yet destroyed the local high school. Each little town had their own school and their own team. It was a sense of pride to the townsfolk, and you could become a legend if you led your high school team to a district or regional championship. If you have watched the movie "Hoosiers," you know exactly what I am talking about. People loved their high school teams and would travel with them as they competed against other small rival towns in the surrounding area. It was simple, and it was fun.

One other note on entertainment – unorganized active sports participation was big back then. When we were young, we played neighborhood pick-up football, basketball and baseball. We would go bowling on weekends, swim on summer days - I even frequented a really nice pool hall when I was in high school. For youngsters you had little league baseball, football, and grade school basketball. But unlike today, you weren't toting kids to practice every day. You practiced once-a-week and then played a game or two. Most of our sports activities were neighborhood pick-up games, not organized practices or games. You weren't "coached" until you started playing ball for the local grade/high school. For young adults, there were some organized leagues, but again, neighborhood pick-up games were the norm. For girls, sports were not much of an option except for swimming and tennis. They concentrated on cheer-leading and dancing for the most part. Overall, we got a lot of exercise and had a lot of fun, much of it spontaneously. That picture has faded into obscurity today.

One other thing to note about content was that entertainment revolved around the family. You did things with your relatives and neighbors. At least in rural settings, weddings were huge and began with the ceremony in the morning and continued late into the night with a dinner and dance. It was literally an all-day affair. Everyone came to celebrate. As mentioned earlier, holidays were huge. All the relatives would meet at Grandma and Grandpa's to celebrate the specific holiday. (New Year's Day, Memorial Day, Independence Day, Labor Day, Thanksgiving, and Christmas.) High school activities were important, and the high school had about as many dances as they had pep rallies. Entertainment was local and meaningful.

What a major difference experiencing entertainment is today. In actuality, entertainment is now 24/7. Practically every person has a small computer that is attached to their hand in today's America. With the tap of a finger you can watch or listen to practically anything you want, be it live or recorded. Technology has enabled us to know what is going on in the world instantaneously, and to have access to video/audio recordings whenever we desire. Content has practically no limitation. Technology has snaked its way into the souls of America. There are many today who can't exist without that computer attached to their hand. And it is everywhere and affects everybody. I was at the gym recently working on some basketball drills when a 20-something guy came in to practice kicking his soccer ball against the wall. He would kick a few and then there would be short pause. I looked up from my drill-work to see why there were periodic pauses in his workout, when I discovered that his phone had never left his hand! He was kicking while looking at his phone's screen. I have no clue as to what he was looking at on that screen, but I know it wasn't a soccer drill he was trying to follow. It was a text or video game or the like. Are you kidding me – you can't spend 30 minutes in a gym practicing your kicks without constantly checking your phone? Now I realize that this example would not normally be considered entertainment, but what else would it be other than this kid entertaining himself with something other than practicing his soccer skills.

Moving beyond the absurd realization that 24/7 technology has possessed people today, let's look at entertainment from a bigger picture. I'll start from where I started with the 50's example – radio. Radio is an interesting medium. It has changed significantly, but has also stayed the same. You can still tune into a station and listen to music, news, or talk-radio (long gone are the drama and comedies of old). There are still commercial breaks on some stations. There are still different genres of music available. Now, however, for a fee you can access the specific type of program/music you want to listen to without any commercial breaks (XM radio, Pandora, etc.). I personally believe this is a real positive improvement in our listening entertainment opportunities. The only downside for me is that I am forced to credit this opportunity to listen at anytime, anywhere, to the computer attached to my hand!

As mentioned above, radio content has changed some. No more "entertainment type" programs like "The Lone Ranger" – instead "talk-radio" has become an entertainment model in itself. Many, many folks spend hours each day listening to talk-radio, be it sports-oriented, politically-oriented, etc. The Rush Limbaugh's of the world have made a living out of hosting call-in programs. Just when you thought radio was dead, along came Rush and hosts similar to him and radio was put back on the map. Bottom line, radio is still entertainment, but its entertainment content has changed significantly.

TV is the next vehicle to dissect. It, also, is somewhat like radio. Some things are still the same, but many things have significantly changed. TV used to be free. In days past you put an antenna on your roof and you could normally get the three main networks (CBS, NBC, and ABC) on your home TV for free. (You had to listen to the advertising, but at least you did not have to pay a fee to do so.) Those days are pretty much gone. Now you pay for a cable or satellite connection in order to watch TV (e.g., Spectrum, Direct TV, etc.). There are still commercials that hunker you down, but many subscription fees include being able to record a program and watch it later. When you do so, you can skip through the commercials. Other options include live streaming of programs directly onto your TV from the computer attached to your hand (e.g., Netflix, Hulu, YouTube, etc.). Today, instead of being limited to three major networks and the programs they decided to broadcast, you have an almost infinite number of programs to watch, depending upon who or what you subscribe to. This, as you would guess, is both good and bad, in my opinion. There are many options to watch educational or entertaining programs from all the various "feeds" available today. There are also many programs not worthy of being recorded that are not only available to you but also to your unsupervised child. Personally I am glad that I am too old to have children at home – monitoring their use of television, internet and their computer attached to their hand would be impossible, I believe. We no longer can control what they are being exposed to on a daily basis. I'll comment on that in another section of the book.

Record players are a thing of the past, although presidential candidate Joe Biden didn't seem to think so as recently as 2020. I have read that vinyl records are making a comeback, but the days of playing a record, even if it is an LP, are gone. With today's technology, it is too easy to listen to exactly what you want and when you want it for the days of "placing a disc on a turntable" to return. Music still entertains people, but their method of listening has changed. Earbuds and music subscriptions are here to stay.

Movie theatres are still alive. It is still fun to go watch a film on the big screen. However, with the other options now available to stream it or subscribe to movies through your TV connection, movie theatres are not as popular. With the advent of the large screen TVs, watching a movie at home isn't quite as good as watching it at the theatre, but it is pretty doggone close. Technology has certainly changed movies, but I think an even bigger change has been to the content of movies. Gone are the censorship days. You can watch practically anything you want today. Murder, sex, drugs, greed, pornography – you name it, it is available somewhere. I have to believe we are not better as a society due to the lack of discipline and decency that has stemmed from the movie industry. What used to be wholesome entertainment has turned into a cesspool. Again, monitoring or controlling the availability of this content is very challenging for parents. No wonder our children are a mess even before reaching their teen years.

Oh, and drive-in movies are practically non-existent. They have all turned into flea markets.

This does not necessarily fall under TV entertainment as we knew it growing up, but it does have something to do with watching something on a screen. Video games. The closest thing we had to video games when I was young was board games. Monopoly, Sorry, The Game of the States, Battle Ship, Scrabble and Yahtzee were some of the most popular games. We pulled them out when we couldn't go outside to play. Today's youngsters now use the computer attached to their hand to play video games. It started when video parlors offered games like Pacman, Donkey Kong, Galaga, Centipede, Battle Zone, etc. As technology advanced, these types of games were available at home using X-Box or some other inexpensive accessory you could connect to your TV. Eventually these options made their way to the computers attached to your hand. Now when you see a child with their parent eating at a restaurant, you see the parent using the computer attached to their hand to send emails, texts or peruse Facebook or Twitter. Meanwhile, the child's attention is glued to their screen which displays Candy Crush, Fortnite, Pokémon Go, or Clash of Clans.

Adults have joined in on the gaming addiction. Men, especially, get hooked on grabbing their X-box or PlayStation and spend hours on end in their "Man Cave" playing NBA 2K22, Fortnite or FIFA22. Or, they may escape totally by putting on their Oculus headset and head off into the world of Virtual Reality. Again, to me it appears that we are settling for fake experiences instead of real life experiences. Regardless, that is where we are today in the world of personal entertainment.

Moving on, sports have become big-time entertainment sources. Pro and some college sports, with their marriage to the TV networks, have overtaken the country. Many males have turned Sports into a god. They feel like they have committed a grave sin if they happen to miss ESPN's Sports Center. This change in our society was gradual, but consistent. We have gone from Baseball's "Saturday Game of the Week" to today's "Every Game Every Minute." You can literally watch every pro baseball, basketball and football game somewhere on TV if you want. (It may cost you an arm and a leg, so to speak, but all these games are available.) The money that this has generated for players, owners, media, etc. is obscene. Plus, it has now presented a platform for any nit-wit athlete to make an uneducated comment on any topic and within 30 seconds you will be aware of these comments. And what is worse, some fans actually listen to these fools. (Not all athletes are uninformed, but I really don't need to hear about how bad it is for some parts of our society from a person who lives in a $10M mansion and has three or four sports cars and a summer get-away home.)

The greed that has been nurtured in both college and pro sports has ruined the game. Seasons now extend so long that there are times when pro baseball, football, basketball, hockey and soccer are all playing at the same time. Playing the World Series in November is nuts, as is playing the NBA Championship in June and the Super Bowl in mid-February. The regular season has so many games that the athletes can't possibly play hard in every game and expect to physically make it to the play-offs. The possibility of injury is astronomical due to the number of games played, and the quality of games is diminished.

Why so many games? Why such a long play-off with extended brackets? Money. Greed. What used to be entertaining is now boring, at least at the pro level. College sports are not far behind, either. There is something wrong when you pay the president of a college $300K - $500K per year and pay the head football or basketball coach $5M or more per year. It is all about money, and you see the same schools at the top of the heap when playing for national championships. I repeat, it is all about money. The days of colleges being amateurs are over, and the entertainment value of watching the same teams compete for national titles is boring.

For college sports, this is only going to get worse. With the new rules allowing athletes to get paid to play and allowing free agency (Name, Image and Likeness rules plus the Transfer Portal, respectively), the rich will get richer and the poor will get poorer. You had seen the beginning of this a few years ago when a player was allowed to transfer to another school if they graduated but still had a year of eligibility remaining. Most of the top teams in the country had at least one "graduate transfer." With the new rules, if a player wants to transfer to another school for any reason, they put their name in the transfer portal pool and are allowed to be recruited by any other school. In addition, non-school personnel can pay the player for using their name, image or likeness. These opportunities include any business engagements where the athlete is compensated for their name, image or likeness.

A local example for me was a good player who played basketball this past year for Kansas State University. I believe he was a sophomore, and he entered the transfer portal this spring and was signed by Miami (FL) University. Interestingly, he was also given $400,000/year for the next two years by a Miami University alum to use the player's name, image and likeness. Basically the players will now be paid to play, and colleges will recruit the best players from other schools. The schools with rich boosters will pay top dollar for the best players from other schools, so colleges will now be "buying" championships.

Unfortunately local sports are not considered by many as entertainment any more. Go to a small college or high school game – there is practically no one in the stands. People stay home and watch sports on TV instead of getting out and cheering on the local team. In the late 60's when I played college basketball for St. Benedict's College (now Benedictine College), an NAIA school of less than 1000 men, we played our rival, Rockhurst University, another all-men school of less than 1000, at Municipal Auditorium in downtown KC. We put 6000 - 8000 people in the seats for that rivalry game.

Today you would be lucky to get 60 - 80 people to show up to watch BC and RU. The same is true for high schools. There are some who have a rabid following, but most play in empty gyms or stadiums. Where are the fans? What has happened to the entertainment value of local teams? I guess if you are not on Sports Center, you are not worth watching and supporting.

I will say that pro sports in smaller markets can still provide some entertainment value and can receive support from the local fan base. Here in KC, where I live, locals love the Chiefs and the Royals. Most of the players live in KC, which helps promote support for the teams. Many players are active in the community. Other small market locations (Green Bay, San Antonio, Charlotte, Jacksonville, Milwaukee, etc.) have similar rabid fan bases, but even there, watching games on TV trumps going to the park to see a live game, even if the tail-gating isn't quite the same! This is a major change from the days before ubiquitous TV coverage.

The other avenue for entertainment in the past has also suffered, i.e., the family. I talked about this in a previous chapter. Because families are no longer co-located in many situations, opportunities for getting together and enjoying each other's company are fewer today. There are some exceptions, but many of today's children grow up and take jobs in places that are a long distance from "home." Some come back to visit periodically, but my experience has been that the children expect the parents to come visit them instead of vice-versa. The product of this new trend is that large extended family get-togethers are the exception instead of the norm today. The downside is not only the loss of an entertainment avenue, but also the loss of close relationships between aunts, uncles, nephews, nieces and first cousins. Family heritage is disintegrating before our eyes. In my opinion, this is a big negative.

So what are my takeaways from this experience?

1. *Observational entertainment is much more available and enjoyable.* My overall take on "Entertainment" today vs. yesterday is that observational entertainment is much more available and enjoyable due to live availability and instant replays and the like.
2. *Active entertainment has suffered greatly.* Today it is all about the appearance of having a good time instead of actually experiencing a good time. As an example, it used to be that you joined friends or relatives to do things together and have a great time. Today, you go with a friend or two to some venue and take a "selfie" of yourselves (with the computer attached to your hand) supposedly having a good time. That is not a healthy trend.
3. *Technology has significantly changed entertainment.* Content has drastically changed for TV and movies, much for the worse. We need to reevaluate what is morally appropriate and what is not, like was done in the early years of TV.

Chapter 9 – Comedy

I am not sure it has always been this way, but observing comedy in a society can really tell you a lot about just where that society is today and probably where it is headed. Comedy is not easy to create, in my opinion. I believe that most really good comics are geniuses. They seem to be a step ahead of most other people mentally, and have the unique ability to tap into things that cause us to think, contemplate, and laugh at our circumstances or ourselves.

Growing up we were blessed with a multitude of comic geniuses. Abbot and Costello's "Who's on First" is one of the funniest things I have ever watched. It is as funny today as it was 70 years ago. Now that is a sign of comedic genius. The Marx Brothers, Milton Berle, The Three Stooges, Art Carney & Jackie Gleason, Sid Caeser, Bob Hope & Bing Crosby, Dean Martin & Jerry Lewis, Lucille Ball & Desi Arnez; the list is long and impressive. What is most impressive to me, though, is that these comedic wonders did so without having to refer to sex or race or anything else that is inappropriate or divisionary. The closest they came to dividing us is when their routines included husband-wife stories, which in most cases were actually truisms that we would acknowledge and be forced to laugh about. The styles of these comics differed significantly – some were TV or movie comics, while some were stand-up comedians. It didn't matter – the content was something you were not embarrassed for your young children to hear.

That trend continued on into the 70's and early 80's when people like Bob Newhart, Bill Cosby, Peter Sellers, Carole Burnette, Dom Deluise, Andy Kaufman, Gene Wilder, and others displayed their talents before us. Excuse the phrase, but their comedy was "good, clean fun." One of my favorites of all time is Rodney Dangerfield – I can listen to him for hours and not stop laughing. The man was crazy-good. Late night host Johnny Carson brought many to a pleasant end of the day experience with his monologues. He was clever, funny, and never mean. Everyone was fair game, and he was never malicious. He had the unique ability of making fun of something someone did, then turn around a few nights later and had them on his show as guests. Comedy was meant to make us laugh back then, not tear down someone else.

Times have changed drastically as far as comedy is concerned. The innocence is gone. Now many comics are simply character assassins. Listen now to late night hosts – they all have a political agenda, and they are ruthless. It is no longer good natured making fun of something someone has done or said. Instead, it is a pointed accusation of someone's stupidity, lack of political correctness, or character flaws. When Jimmy Fallon first took over for Jay Leno (who was funny in the Carson mold), he was actually fun to watch. Then something happened, and he became politically motivated and his routines became mean and hateful, especially if you lean conservative in your views. We stopped watching and have never turned him back on since then. Why end your day with people being mean and hurtful. There is enough of that going around during the day and you certainly don't need more of it before retiring to bed.

The other major change is the content itself. Today's comedy writers are incapable of creating content that is clean and wholesome. Every joke or every sit-com is full of sexual innuendoes or political prejudice. Can you imagine today's writers being able to produce just one show of "I Love Lucy?" They can't – they aren't talented enough – they have to refer back to sex or political correctness. Watch an old Andy Griffith TV show, and tell me if Don Knotts' character "Barney Fife" isn't hilarious – and not one episode had Barney doing anything that your 8-year old couldn't watch. Today, there is practically no show your 8-year old can watch. There will be referrals to sex, gay/lesbianism/transgenderism, foul language, etc. that you simply don't want your child to be exposed to at that age.

So when did this change happen? Well, like so many other things, it was gradual. We allow "this to be okay," then "that to be okay," and eventually the pendulum has moved all the way to the other side. Comedy was a victim of this gradual slide. I'm sure that some of the old comics, in their personal appearances in live concerts, were somewhat risqué at times. However, you never saw that on broadcast media. I loved listening to Richard Pryor. He was so funny, but you couldn't take one of his concerts and put it on TV.

They were too vulgar. TV shows like Seinfeld, Sex and the City, and Two and a Half Men moved the needle of what was acceptable on TV. Over time, practically anything is now okay. Some of that is due to the relaxation of the censorship rules by the major networks, but most is probably due to the availability of cable channels and now live streaming. Who is going to police all these entry points? The answer is "parents." No one else is going to step up and limit what you or your children can watch or listen to these days. It is up to you to discipline yourself and supervise your children. Neither of those things are easy, but both are required if we want to continue to live in a respectable society.

So what are my takeaways from this experience?

1. *Good, wholesome comedy is very hard to find.* Comic content has changed so dramatically that it has become very difficult to find comedy that the whole family can watch together. Writers take the easy way out and rely on sex, race, political agendas and the like to create content. Until this changes, comedy will continue on its downward spiral.

Chapter 10 – Travel

In the 50's and 60's travel was something that was more of a chore than something fun to do. President Eisenhower had just started developing the interstate highway system, so most roads in the U.S. were two lane highways at best. The speed limit was normally 55 mph and every highway made its way through a small town about every 8 miles or so where the speed limit was 30. It took forever to get anywhere, especially if you got stuck behind a semi-truck and couldn't pass it due to oncoming traffic.

It was during these years that I thought I would be dead before reaching my teens. It seemed like there was always a head-on collision locally and people died. My dad exacerbated my fears – he was a maniac on the highway. I can't tell you how many times we were in the car staring out from the back seat as he was passing a vehicle while another vehicle was just seconds from hitting us head-on. If there was a crack available to pass, dad took it. Fortunately, God protected us during that period of my fragile life – the closest we came to crashing was one-time when he tried to pass a car and couldn't make it back into our lane. We were three-abreast on a two-lane highway going 70 miles an hour, our car being in the middle. It was frighteningly horrible. I was ecstatic when I turned 16 and got my driver's license – not so much because I was now mobile and could "cruise" the hamburger shops, but more so that I now did not have to ride with my dad except on special occasions.

Auto travel was slow and cumbersome so many folks took shorter trips to go on vacation. Driving from Ohio to, say, Florida or Colorado took too long, so most people would drive to Tennessee or Michigan to vacation. The same was true for going to the big city. Going to Cleveland or Cincinnati was about 120 miles from our home town, but getting there would take 3 or 4 hours. We seldom made it to the big towns, which meant shopping, entertainment, etc. was localized.

Trains were still a big thing back then. Rather than drive to Chicago, it was much easier (and cheaper) to take a passenger train. They weren't necessarily faster than driving (due to the number of stops in towns along the way), but they were very comfortable and extremely safe. Plus, you had multiple choices as to when you could catch a train – you weren't limited to just one train a day. Greyhound busses were also available if you wanted an even cheaper option than a train, but they were not as comfortable. They also made more stops than the train and their route was a little more serpentine, so they weren't as efficient time-wise as a train or car.

Air-travel was a luxury. Jet engines were just being introduced nationally in 1959, so many of the flights were on planes which had either two or four gas-powered piston engines. Planes flew at lower altitudes back then because of the type of engines used, and periodically you would read about a plane hitting the side of a mountain and everyone perishing. I was not in a big hurry to fly back in those days – it was about as safe as riding with my dad in his car!

As Pan American Airlines and others rolled out the new Boeing 707s and Douglas's DC-8s, jet plane travel exploded. It was still much more expensive to fly than to take a train, bus, or car, but you could get places extremely fast compared to other means of travel. Now going to Disneyland (Disneyworld was not built yet) was a four or five hour plane ride to California instead of a 3 or 4 day drive. As long as you could afford the plane tickets, a whole new world of vacationing was opened up to America. This, along with the completion of a major part of the Interstate Highway System, created a new mobility in our country. Times were good, and still are today. (However, the airline industry has hit a bump in the road recently, with a shortage of pilots and air traffic controllers. Many flights are being cancelled leaving passengers stranded and scrambling for replacement flights. Plus, due to the country's energy policies, fuel costs have increased causing the ticket prices for travelers to also increase.)

In today's world, transportation options are so much better than when I grew up, as explained above. Now you don't have the train option you used to have, and bus schedules and their destinations are very limited. But auto travel is very easy, inexpensive, and efficient. Even if you don't own a car, you can still take advantage of this means of transportation by renting or leasing a vehicle. Flying, although it has become a huge hassle since 9/11, is very efficient and available. With multiple airlines flying multiple flights to most big cities around the country, you have your choice of when and where to fly at a very reasonable price. And it is a safe method of travel.

What the improvement in travel options has done is to allow our country to be much more mobile. In most cases, that is a good thing. Almost everyone benefits from this – business, industry, entertainment, etc. The only down side, from my perspective as mentioned above, is that families are not co-located anymore and that affects the myriad of things I will address in the "Family" chapter.

So what are my takeaways from this experience?

1. *Travel has improved significantly over the years.* We are so much better off today than in the past as far as travel is concerned. Interstate highways and jet plane service have significantly improved our ability to see loved ones and things of interest that were difficult to access in the past.

Chapter 11 - Exercise & Health

I can't really say we were healthier in the 50's and 60's as opposed to today – there were many things that caused sickness and death that we were unaware of from a medical perspective. However, even with all the medical technology and innovations that have become available today, people are still ill or dying when they need not be. Even ignoring the Coronavirus pandemic of the last couple of years, the world does not appear to be getting healthier. Cancer has not been solved, and heart disease actually is responsible for more deaths each year than cancer. They are the two biggies. Strokes and Alzheimer's are significant causes of death too. Back in my day growing up, people got Parkinson's and had strokes and heart attacks, but most died of "old age." Dementia and Alzheimer's were around, but they were not called that. Most often we referred to this as "hardening of the arteries." These were considered "old age" causes, even though old age was considered being in your late 60's or early 70's. It was probably true in many cases that your body just wore out back then. People worked hard, be it on the farm or in the factory. Hours were long and physical work was demanding. Many men simply wore out. I'm sure diet had something to do with it, and lack of specific medical treatment and prevention probably also contributed to an earlier death. But the physical side of work was much more demanding in the 50's and 60's than it is today. Robotics and technology have certainly changed the way we work.

One of the reasons I believe that our health has not improved is diet and lack of exercise. From a dietary standpoint, America devours tons of sugar. It is in everything, as is salt. Think about your family and friends and consider how many are practically addicted to soft drinks. They constantly have a "Big Gulp" in their hand (opposite the computer attached to the other hand) and will order a "coke" or better yet, a "diet coke," whenever they order something to eat. At night they sit in front of the TV and drink more coke or beer, neither of which helps your health one iota. Fast food is full of sugar and salt, as is the processed food that we eat for lunch or dinner. Trying to eat a healthy diet is practically impossible unless you are

Oprah and have a live-in chef. Some people are disciplined enough to eat right most of the time, but they are few and far between. That is the reason why so many people die from heart disease and other inflammatory diseases. I mentioned the coronavirus above – how many people died from already being in bad health before they contracted the virus? (Unfortunately, we won't know, because our government decided to classify all deaths as Covid deaths even if a person was in their last days due to cancer or heart disease. If you think I am exaggerating, look at the stats for 2019-2020 for people who died from the flu versus previous years. Amazingly, for a year or two we eradicated the flu.)

Exercise is the other factor involved in America's health. We as a country are obese. Diet generates it, and lack of exercise maintains it. When I was growing up, occasionally you had overweight people. Today, just stand at the entrance to Wal-Mart or watch people walk by in a restaurant. Count the number who are not fat. You won't have to be a mathematician to keep track. I will count at least four out of every five people who pass me by as being fat. Not just overweight – fat, or maybe even obese, with rolls around their stomachs, hips and legs. Many, many men look pregnant. Women don't walk by, they waddle by. Although some people may have a medical condition causing this, most look this way due to dietary choices and lack of exercise. There is no way to burn the excess calories needed to maintain a healthy weight, so our weight continues to increase. Unfortunately, the older we get, the harder it is for us to burn the required calories to stay in shape. To achieve that requires us to eat less (or healthier) and/or exercise more.

Growing up we did not have fast food places on every corner or QuikTrips on the other three corners. If you wanted a soft drink, you had to find a vending machine and hope you had the correct change. You ate breakfast at home, had lunch at a local diner, and were back home for supper. The quality of the food was usually pretty good, because it was home grown and herbicides and pesticides were in their infancy. Quite a bit of the food was fried, which wasn't necessarily good, but they used "lard" to fry the food and not hydrogenated vegetable shortening (trans fat), which causes heart disease. People had jobs that required physical exercise, so they would burn off breakfast and lunch each day. At night, after supper you didn't plop your fat butt down on the couch, open up a beer or two, grab some chips and watch Baywatch reruns. Instead, you probably retired to your favorite chair, grabbed a book/magazine or listened to the radio, maybe had a glass of milk or some decaf, and then retired early to bed because you knew you had a hard day's work ahead of you the next day. Snacks just didn't enter the equation. Soft drinks were not hyped (advertised) in order to make you feel cool if you had one in your hand (either hand, since this pre-dated the computer that is attached to the modern human hand).

One thing that has improved over the years is the number of Americans who smoke. When I was young, it seemed like most adults smoked. Both mom and dad smoked in our home. People smoked at work, in restaurants, at sporting events (even inside), etc. For men, "The Marlboro Man" was Mr. Cool in TV and billboard ads. Billboards were saturated with Camels, Lucky Strike, and Pall Mall ads. "Kool" was a lighter cigarette geared toward women (and light weights, according to Camel smokers). Movies and TV shows included actors and actresses lighting up their "Winston." It was considered normal. In fact, many kids in high school were considered "cool" if they smoked. About the only place it was prohibited was on high school or college sports teams. You could be booted off the team if you were caught smoking. Ironically, one of the reasons that generation was thinner than today's generation was due to smoking. (New studies show that nicotine works in the brain to suppress smokers' appetites.)

Fortunately, habits have changed and fewer people smoke today than in my growing up years. Studies linking smoking to cancer have caused many people either to stop smoking or to never start. That is a good thing. Rules and regulations limiting where you can smoke have also been a contributing factor to the reduction in smoking. Education and awareness have influenced people's behavior for the good. Let's just hope that the new "vaping" trend does not reverse the progress that has been made.

As far as exercise is concerned, gyms were not very available, unless you were a serious body-builder. Your work was normally enough exercise to keep you fit. In addition, if you had energy left over at the end of the day, you might go bowling or play in a baseball or softball league in town. Treadmills were unheard of, as were elliptical machines and the like. If you wanted a cardio workout, you put on your "tenna-shoes" and ran a couple of miles. You might have a set of weights in your basement to try to keep buffed up a little, but taking the time to go to a gym to lift was only for guys who wanted to compete in body-building contests. Women didn't go to gyms. I'm really not sure what they did to stay in shape outside of working at home, but they must have privately danced or swam or something after graduating from high school. Looking back on it, it is pretty amazing that people were in as good of shape as they were, considering that today, unlike then, we have all these opportunities to workout. I believe that the better diet and physical work itself were responsible for the results.

Today we have so many opportunities to stay in good physical condition, but few take advantage of those opportunities. I have mentioned how poorly we eat – no need to delve further into that subject – thousands of books have documented that fact. As far as exercise is concerned, there are two problems I see with today's environment. First, people don't have time to go to the gym. Young folks are busy with career pursuits and personal entertainment, and young parents are too busy steering the SUV to the next kids' practice. Older folks are too comfortable having not exercised for years as they were rearing their families and now have little or no interest in doing something that taxes their bodies.

The second thing I feel that keeps people from getting into good physical condition is attitude – what is the real reason for working out? So many do it for the wrong reasons. It is not to stay healthy, but rather to "look good" or be a part of the social scene. Don't misunderstand me – there are men and women who are serious about their health and how they maintain their bodies. I am always impressed with those who show up on a regular basis and lift weights, do the stair-climber, or run on the treadmill. Others have a strict regimen of walking or jogging daily. I am not referring to these men and women – I applaud them. Rather, I am talking about the women who go to a short Zumba class and then call it a day by jumping into their SUV and stopping by their local Starbucks on the way home to buy a Cinnamon Roll Frappuccino Blended Coffee. (Maybe their second of the day.) Men will go to the gym and lift a few weights while staring at the best edition of yoga pants being happily displayed by one of the female stair climber or treadmill users. And who sweats anymore? To stay in shape, you have to work hard. I've always felt that if I didn't sweat during a workout, I might as well have not worked out. Now I am not saying that I accomplish this every time I work out, but it is my goal. Without this daily commitment, I find myself quickly drifting toward 190 pounds and a cute little roll around the belly! (To be transparent, some of my friends think I obsess over working out daily. They are probably right.)

Bottom line, there are some people who are serious about their health and the amount of exercise they get each day. As mentioned above, I applaud these people. Unfortunately, in the U.S. this may be 10 – 20% of the adult population. (I realize that for some not included in this group, they may have medical or physical issues that prevent them from exercising daily.) Disease, injuries and illnesses will continue to grow if this trend continues. What may be even more concerning is what we are doing to our children and grandchildren. Have you noticed how fat they are getting? Again, you can trace it back to diet and exercise. Kids' diets are packed full of sugar. Fast food is consumed at a high rate, and soft drinks are like water to the younger set. "Back in the day" when kids got home from school and immediately went out to play with their friends is now, effectively, "back in the day." (However, one of the positive benefits of parents having to be Uber SUV drivers for their children after school taking them to "ball" practice is that at least the kids get some exercise during these after-school adventures.) When was the last time you saw kids playing in the driveway or at the local playground? Today's kids, who are born with a computer attached to their hand, stumble home while trying to read whatever is on the screen in their hand. When arriving home, they plop on the couch and use both hands to manipulate the keys on the screen in their hand. They will sit there for hours until one of the parents comes home with a sack full of fast food for supper. This scenario plays out day after day. Unless this changes, our country is in for a health disaster within the next generation. Regardless of the new drugs developed to fight obesity and other illnesses, our future generations will be significantly less healthy than past generations. We must change!

[As an aside, I think there is a spiritual responsibility we have for our health as well as the practical things I have discussed in this chapter. I believe that God has given each of us specific gifts with an expectation that we will use these gifts to glorify Him. Some people are gifted musically, others athletically, others analytically, etc. One specific gift that He gives to all of us, though, is our body. I believe He expects us to develop it just as He expects us to develop our other specific unique gifts. I believe that when we die and are facing Our Lord, He will ask us to evaluate how well we have developed and used all of the gifts He gave us at birth, including our body. Did we take care of it, or did we ignore or abuse it? I don't mean that He expects us to work out all the time and look like some movie star – but rather did we eat right? Did we get consistent exercise? Did we nourish it so that it would be a help in glorifying Him in our work, play and relationships? Or did we neglect it and make it an albatross in accomplishing His purpose for each of us? I think this is a question that each of us should ask ourselves often. And like anything else as it concerns God, it is never too late to change ourselves and follow His will.]

So what are my takeaways from this experience?

1. *America is in for some bad times health-wise*. We are not disciplined when it comes to food or exercise. We have programmed our younger people to be addicted to salt and sugar. We are an obese nation with no sense of desiring change. Pardon my French, but we are screwed.
2. *There is a spiritual side to health as well as a practical side*. Making a spiritual commitment to physically nurture our bodies will go a long way in helping us achieve healthy outcomes.

Chapter 12 – Healthcare

I am not exactly sure if we had health insurance or not when I was growing up. What I do know is that the local Delphos doctor, in my case Dr. Illig, made frequent house calls. Again, I am not sure how he determined when and who to see in the privacy of their own home. Doc Illig had a schedule whereby he would drive to your home and treat you for whatever ailed you. We lived on a farm at the time, so the good doctor had to drive into the country to come see us. In case of an emergency, you could call for an ambulance, drive into town to see your doctor, or drive to the "big town" to the hospital emergency room.

My recollection is that we paid cash for the services at the time they were administered. In the 50's a little over half the U.S. population had private health insurance. The rest of the folks paid cash for the service. By 1970, about four out of every five people in the U.S. had private health insurance. For many, it was a "perk" that companies used to attract and retain more qualified employees. As an incentive provided by the government to employers, employer-sponsored health insurance received tax-exempt status. Unions also got in on the act, using health insurance as a collective bargaining chip. These factors drove the significant increase in the number of U.S. citizens who had private health insurance.

With the enactment of Medicare in 1965, older Americans were now able to have health insurance after completing their work life. In 1974 the Employment Retirement Income Security Act (ERISA) allowed self-insured employer health plans. It became competition for the conventional insurance market. Then in the 80's and 90's Medicaid and Medicare were radically expanded. Children under 19 became eligible, plus, prescription drugs were included in the coverage.

In the 2000's, tax-sheltered health spending accounts were introduced. In 2010, the Patient Protection and Affordable Care Act (Obamacare) was passed forcing individuals to purchase health insurance or be fined. All of these governmental interventions caused the number of citizens covered by health insurance plans to expand dramatically over time. (It also caused record-keeping to become a nightmare for employers and the medical industry.)

From the above chronological narrative you can see just how drastically health insurance has changed. Back in my growing up years, healthcare was affordable – people paid cash for services and doctors were patient oriented. In my opinion, this all changed when the lawyers (malpractice suits) and government (Medicare, Medicaid, Obamacare) got involved. People in our day did not go to the doctor unless they were really sick – they simply couldn't afford to go every time they had a runny nose. Doctors and hospitals, in turn, did not charge exorbitant amounts for simple office visits and minor surgeries. As insurance plans expanded and the insurance companies got involved in reimbursing doctors a set amount for specific services and procedures, prices and service started to go in opposite directions. Enter the ambulance chasers and add the feds to the equation and now you have what we have today – runaway healthcare costs.

Healthcare itself has come a long way. In my day robots were what you saw in the sci-fi flicks on Saturday afternoons – they had nothing to do with medical procedures. A doctor with a set of X-rays, a steady hand and significant experience was what we all counted on to get top level treatment for our injuries and ills. Today, with the tremendous advances in technology, not only surgical procedures are significantly improved, but also diagnostics are off the chart. MRI's, CT scans, ultrasounds, etc. provide physicians with information that was not available back when I grew up. This has both sped up the diagnosis process and improved its accuracy. Americans are now in a better position to be treated for a serious illness or injury sooner and more effectively today.

The serious downside that I see to healthcare is from a drug perspective. I believe the medical profession has become drug dominant. It seems like every time you go to the doctor for whatever ails you, a new prescription is written and you start taking a drug that is supposed to resolve your medical issue. Add to that the fact that the profession has become extremely specialized, and you have one doctor not knowing what another doctor has prescribed for you. There can be, and often is, a negative reaction to taking multiple drugs. Managing that has fallen upon the individual, with the help of his/her pharmacist or personal physician. This can be a daunting task for some, especially those who had contracted cancer and are taking a large number of drugs to treat the cancer. The fault for taking many drugs can not only be directed towards the physicians but also rests with the patient. Many patients are looking for the "quick fix" and simply want to take a drug and be done with it. Add to that the risk of becoming addicted to certain drugs, and now you've got a serious national problem on your hands.

> [As a side note, prescription drugs as a solution to Americans' ills have become very concerning as it applies to anxiety, depression, mood disorders, psychotic disorders, etc. Practically every time there is a mass shooting, we find out that the shooter has been on some antidepressant or SSRI (Selective Serotonin Reuptake Inhibitors). Young people and adults are on Zoloft, Prozac, Luvox, Xanax, and other SSRI's more than ever before. Tucker Carlson, Fox News' top program host, recently reported that between 1991 and 2018, SSRI prescriptions in the U.S. rose by 3000%. That is 30 more times in 2018 than in 1991! During that same period, suicides increased by 35%. Why do we feel more depressed, anxious and suicidal today than we did years ago? And why aren't these drugs working? I personally believe that our change in lifestyle has caused this. We eat poorly, exercise poorly, spend most of our lives on the computer attached to our hand, fail to create close real-life personal relationships, have no relationship with our Creator, never take the time to pray, have made ourselves the center of existence, and have no hope. That is a formula for disaster, and prescribing more drugs will not make it better.]

I had mentioned in the previous chapter that Americans' eating and exercise habits are the source for many, many serious diseases. As I opined, we have become addicted to sugar and salt (me included), and now large amounts of the population are dealing with hypertension, diabetes and heart problems. Rather than change our diet and exercise habits, we instead have another prescription written and hope that takes care of the problem. It doesn't in almost all cases. So even though our medical profession is light years ahead of the 50's and 60's, our national health is not. I saw a recent CDC statistic (2017 – 2018) that over 19% of children and 42% of adults are obese. Not just fat, but obese! Processed foods and sugar are the culprits. Cancer and cardiovascular disease are the result. (I read an article by Dr. Joseph Mercola stating that over the past 200 years our sugar intake has risen from 2 pounds/year to 152 pounds/year.) If we don't change our life styles, this trend will simply grow worse.

Our healthcare system today is financially and organizationally broken. It is hard for people to exist without healthcare insurance and you almost have to have a second job to pay for it. Government intrusion into the healthcare system has caused prices to skyrocket. Everything is regulated. Even at that, malpractice lawsuits flourish. Doctors can't afford to have their own practices anymore. Equipment and insurance are too expensive, so that a physician must belong to a hospital group who then dictates how long they spend with each patient and how much they charge for their services. Bottom line has become more important than patient outcomes. That is not how it was back in my days growing up.

So what are my takeaways from this experience?

1. *Technology has driven tremendous progress*. From a knowledge and available treatment view, we are much better off today than in the 50's and 60's.
2. *Customer service has suffered greatly*. Due to the risk involved in being a doctor and the change brought about by hospitals now "owning" physicians, customer service has declined.
3. *Costs have increased*. Americans are less disciplined when it comes to diet and exercise, causing additional pressure on the healthcare system. Government intrusion has taken away the flexibility and affordability doctors used to have. Costs are unaffordable without insurance today.

4. *Prescription drugs are out of control.* Whenever we have something wrong, we and the medical community both rely too heavily on prescription drugs to "fix" things. We must find a way to break that cycle and return to living a well-balanced life physically, mentally and spiritually.

Chapter 13 - Race Relations

When people speak of race relations, they normally mean black-white relations. America has had its issues with other races before, including Native Americans, Mexicans and the Japanese (WW II), but during my childhood the primary big divide was between blacks and whites. Growing up I really didn't know any black kids until I got to high school and started to go to the playgrounds in the black sections of our town to play basketball. Some whites portrayed the blacks as inferior. (My mother, however, showed compassion toward blacks and taught us to treat everyone as equals.) The N-word was used right out in the open by many whites. Blacks were relegated to the poor side of town (south Lima for us), and it was commonly known that you stayed out of those neighborhoods, especially at night. There were a number of black "women of the night" that walked the sidewalks of one of the downtown streets bordering on the southeast part of the city. There was also a "red light district" on the south side of town. I vaguely remember our town still having some restrooms and drinking fountains that were segregated when I was very young, and almost all of the black kids attended Lima Senior Public High School. Even when I was older, I believe we had only three or four blacks in our Catholic High School. It was the same in three of the other four suburban Lima high schools. Getting to personally know someone of a different race was not too easy back then.

Although slavery had ended in 1865, the plight for blacks in the 1950's and 60's was pretty grim. There were a handful of movie stars (Sidney Poitier) and sports stars (Jimmy Brown, Willie Mays, Wilt Chamberlain), but for the most part your chance to succeed in most careers was greatly enhanced if you were white. Then, along came Rosa Parks and Dr. Martin Luther King Jr. and things started to change.

I was in high school when the peaceful marches in the south began, and I watched on television as peaceful marchers were beaten, fire-hosed, and tear-gassed by police in the south. Fortunately, we did not have much of that behavior in Ohio, but you saw it happen on the nightly national news programs and wondered what the hell was going on. It took tremendous courage and emotional restraint on the part of Dr. King and his supporters to push the envelope on civil rights for all Americans. As you know, he ended up being martyred for the cause. But his life was not taken in vain – because of his and others' efforts, including white people, laws and lives were changed.

I was blessed to have a mom who, as an adult, appreciated being free to do whatever white Americans could do. Mom was the daughter of an Italian immigrant, and experienced significant prejudice as a girl growing up in Lima. The Italians were considered second class citizens and treated very poorly. She never forgot that, and she never let us forget that all people are created equal in the eyes of God and should be treated accordingly. She used to call the blacks "colored people." I think it was her way of softening the word Negro, which was too close to the N-word for her. Because of my mom's influence, I had a healthy attitude as it pertained to blacks, and took the risk of going to the black playgrounds to play against some really talented black kids. Interestingly, I don't remember any negative comments from the kids on the playground about me being white – they, like me, just wanted to play ball.

When I went to college in Kansas to study and play basketball, I remember the first day at St. Benedict's College standing in line to enroll. One of the stops in the line was at the dorm assignment table. I was assigned to Freshman Hall (as opposed to the newer St. Michael's Hall). The priest handing out room assignments asked me a question that not only surprised me, but also confused me a little. He said "Your roommate is so-and-so, and he is black. Is that alright with you?" I'm sure I looked puzzled, but I said "Sure." It turned out that my roommate was a player from St. Louis who, like me, had little, if any, experience being around someone from a different race. We both learned a lot that freshman year, and both of us grew substantially in regards to respect for each other's culture.

Fast forward to where we are today in race relations, and you can see that a tremendous amount of progress has been made over two generations. I am not naïve enough to think that prejudice doesn't exist in America, but today blacks have succeeded in many fields. Their opportunities are real today.

We no longer have any outward public signs of prejudice like the ones we had in the 1950's and 60's. America came so far as to elect a half white-half black president, who identified himself as black. Who would have thought when Rosa Parks was arrested for not giving up her seat to a white man on that Montgomery, Alabama bus in 1955 that a little over 50 years later a black man would be elected the President of the United States? It is quite amazing and refreshing – Americans did the right thing as it concerned equal rights for all citizens.

I know that there are some folks that will strongly disagree with me concerning current day levels of prejudice. I am not saying that it doesn't exist – what I am saying is that we have come a long way since I was young. Most of those who strongly disagree with me are probably younger people. They have not seen the significantly positive changes that have happened over my lifetime. You can read about it and look at pictures all you want, but being there and experiencing it takes on a whole new perspective. It is like the lyrics from country singer Jamey Johnson's song, describing a conversation he had with his grandpa who had experienced the Great Depression and World War II. Ironically, the name of the song is "You Should've Seen It In Color." Those are the words used by the grandpa while looking with his grandson at old black and white photos of times past. He basically tells the grandson that you had to experience it to know what it was really like. He says:

> "A picture's worth a thousand words
>
> But you can't see what those shades of gray keep covered
>
> You should've seen it in color."

I realize that even though most, if not all, of the outward signs of prejudice are gone, there still exists an unspoken or emotional component that will take longer to resolve. Many blacks, especially younger black males, fear being stopped by the police. They are scared that they will not be treated fairly or be wrongfully charged for something they did not do. They are justified in feeling this way based on some of the incidents that have been reported by news media as well as many incidents that are simply experienced by blacks and are not being reported. Black men are distressed when white ladies clutch their purses out of fear or people lock their car doors due to the perception of a black male being a threat. For a black person, this is unfair, not knowing the character or integrity of that black person. These feelings/emotions will take longer to change for both blacks and whites. Like any other emotion/feeling, when we experience something over and over with the same result, our expectation of that result grows. The distress and fear will diminish when people's experiences of being exposed to one another in these types of situations result in nothing ever happening.

A common theme of today's progressive movement claims that there is "systemic racism" in the U.S. My best interpretation of that term is that there is built in racism in all parts of our society. I disagree strongly with that view. I was there in January 1973 when AT&T signed a "consent decree" with the government's Equal Employment Opportunity Commission (EEOC) to implement an affirmative action plan for women and minorities. It gave priority for jobs and promotions to blacks and women. I saw it time and again over my nearly 30 year career at AT&T where the most qualified white male candidate was passed over in favor of a less qualified black or woman. (This is not to imply that minorities or women were not as smart or as effective as white males. The truth is that neither minorities nor women had the benefit of the education and experience that white males were exposed to back then. Blacks were not accepted into most colleges and universities, and the women that were enrolled followed the "elementary and secondary education" tract in earning their degree in order to become teachers. Extremely few of either of these groups earned degrees in business, marketing, finance, etc. Until college educational opportunities were expanded, there just weren't many black or female college grads that had the educational credentials to be hired into management positions in corporate America.)

We white males who were the recipients of this consent decree did not like being passed over, but most of us understood the reasoning behind it and accepted it. We realized that blacks and women needed to have a policy in place that allowed them to advance within the corporate job market at a more rapid pace so that equality could be achieved sooner. AT&T was the first large corporation to implement such a plan, and it proved to be a successful way of giving minorities and women a way to move into good jobs and move up the corporate ladder. That policy was in for most of my career. Did it hurt my chances of advancement? Yes. Do I hold that against women and minorities? No. I had to look at it from a big picture perspective, and not a selfish individual one. To make significant progress for minorities in all phases of life in the U.S., we had to more than just follow the new Civil Rights Act of 1964, which ended segregation in public places and banned employment discrimination on the basis of race, color, religion, sex or national origin. We had to expedite it, and I'm glad to say that AT&T led the way. Soon, many corporations followed AT&T's actions, and we started to see opportunities open up that had not been available before to minorities and women. This continued for practically my entire career at Bell, so that by the new millennium, affirmative action programs were no longer necessary. The "system" was no longer inbred to favor white males. Thirty years of expedited opportunities was responsible for that.

The idea pushed by many progressives, that whites are born with a built-in prejudice against blacks and vice-versa, is ludicrous. If you are a parent or grandparent, just go to your local childcare facility and watch the toddlers for a while. What you will notice is that none of them show any signs of racial prejudice. The black babies and white babies play together, sometimes sharing toys and sometimes not. When they don't share, color of skin has nothing to do with it. They can't see color when deciding to share a favorite toy with anyone else. It is as simple as the children selfishly wanting the toy for themselves. Period. So this idea of built in prejudice is a lie. Prejudice is a learned behavior.

Likewise, saying that institutions all have built in prejudices is also false in today's America. After nearly 60 years of affirmative action and civil rights progress, America is beyond that. Has prejudice been eliminated in America in 2022? No. There will always be some prejudice – it is part of the human experience. But I believe it is based on the individual, not the institution. People are taught by others to be prejudiced, or maybe they had a bad experience with someone of a different race. There are many reasons why someone might become prejudiced, but it is not inborn – God did not create us with racial prejudice in our hearts. Have we created a utopian environment where no one is a bigot? No. Unfortunately, we as a country will never get there because we as individuals will never get there. There will always be someone who takes advantage of another because they don't like their color or religion or sex. Until Jesus returns to this earth, we will continue to experience that behavior. What we can do, however, is to make sure we never do that ourselves. We should also point out to those who do exhibit such behavior that they are not being unbiased, just or fair with the other individual. It all starts with the individual person – progress will not continue to occur without hearts continuing to change.

I will probably be criticized deeply for this next paragraph, but I feel it needs to be said. Up until Barrack Obama was elected President, I believed things were continuing to move in a positive direction as far as race relations were concerned. Soon after he took office, though, I felt like his actions turned the curve downward. I felt like his actions created a divide in our country, pitting whites against blacks and blacks against whites. His actions and comments concerning the "Beer Summit" controversy, the Trayvon Martin death and the Ferguson, Mo., shooting created a huge division in our country. In my opinion, he did not wait for the facts of the cases to be determined – he assumed that all were cases of racial prejudice and/or police misconduct or brutality against blacks. In doing so, he pitted the blacks against the whites and rather than promote racial harmony, he stoked the fires of racial hatred.

It is a shame that President Obama chose the path he chose – he could have been the shining light of our generation. Had he spent time working to fix the cause of any police misbehavior rather than simply espousing that it was ubiquitous in the U.S., we could have punished those who were guilty of the misbehavior without causing an emotional and physical upheaval that created violent organizations like Black Lives Matter (BLM). Had he spent time working on fixing the problems in the inner cities and giving those people hope of a better existence, the number of black-on-black murders would not have continued to skyrocket. Had he spent time working on public education and promoting school choice and charter schools, think how far ahead of the game today's black 20 year olds would be. But in my opinion, he did not want to unite the country. He wanted "change," and the type of changes he desired could only come about by dividing the country. He was pretty successful in doing so – we now have blacks against whites, conservatives against liberals, gays against straights, non-Christians against Christians, socialists against capitalists, elites against the common man, etc. All of these flames were fueled during President Obama's eight years in office.

Unfortunately, I don't see anyone on the horizon that can reverse this course. Our leadership today in America is extremely weak. Our leaders are that in name only – they know little about true leadership. So few are willing to roll up their sleeves and do the hard work of bringing people together by doing what is right and using common sense. Too many are influenced by big money and the desire for wealth, power and fame. We need a Martin Luther King Jr. or a John Kennedy or a Ronald Reagan.

So, are race relations hopelessly lost? Not necessarily. It must start, however, with the individual. Each person, regardless of color, was created in the image and likeness of God. We each need to be a reflection of our Creator. Each of us must do what is right and just and then hold others accountable for doing the same. We must look at ways of helping our brothers and sisters escape from the quagmire that the governmental social programs have helped cause. We must elect officials who will do the right thing even when their donors do not support it. We must insist upon schools that advance the knowledge, integrity and skills sets of our young people. We must promote and reward fathers who take the leadership position in and the responsibility for the family they have physically created. We must give others hope. That starts with personal sacrifice and commitment. Without such an effort, our country will continue on the downward slope as far as race relations are concerned.

So what are my takeaways from this experience?

1. *America's progress has been derailed.* Due to the changes that occurred in the 50's, 60's and early 70's, America was on the right path to creating a society who treated people equally regardless of their skin color or sex. Due to the "Hope and Change" agenda of

2008 and beyond, the upward trajectory of race relations changed course. We are now on a downward trajectory. Only true leadership, sacrifice and discipline can reverse this course. That must come first from the individual person before it can permeate itself throughout our society.

2. *All is not lost: the negative trend can be reversed.* Looking back, we have come a long way since my growing up years. Today our TV and magazine commercials/ads are significantly populated with blacks, which you never would have seen 60 years ago. Mixed marriages are numerous and more widely accepted, whereas it was unheard of in the 50's and 60's. Blacks have leadership positions in business, government, entertainment, etc. We must not let this progress be for naught. We must work to reverse the course of race-relations and racial division that has been re-introduced in the last decade and a half. We must work together, blacks and whites, to re-establish the progress we have made over the last 60 years. For that to happen, primary and secondary education has to be improved significantly for poor people, especially minorities. The nuclear family has to be re-emphasized and somehow rewarded to encourage significant growth in this area. Drugs and gangs need to be eliminated and a sense of self-worth needs to be developed in our inner cities. The values taught by the local Christian churches need to be adopted and acted out. Just throwing money at it from afar, as the government has done for decades, will not do the trick. Active involvement and leadership will be required, not from the government, but from ordinary citizens.

Chapter 14 - Family

Looking back on my lifetime and observing what has happened to the family is tragic, in my opinion. Back in the 50's family and extended family took priority over everything, except maybe faith.

Back then a family was a man married to a woman, who together produced anywhere from two to ten children. Dad wore the pants in the family and normally was the breadwinner. Mom was the nurturer and normally stayed home and ran the household. There were both love and discipline in a family, although a lot of World War II vets who became fathers did not show their love so much outwardly. Kids were often seen, but not heard. They all had daily chores and some received a weekly allowance. Dad normally worked Monday to Friday, did home repairs and maintenance on Saturdays, and went to church on Sundays with the rest of the family. Moms worked "hard" at home Monday to Friday, doing the laundry, cooking, cleaning the house, and sometimes tending the garden. On Saturdays she shopped for groceries and other family needs, and on Sunday went to church and then cooked a feast for Sunday dinner (noon). The kids went to school Monday to Friday and did their daily chores and school homework. On Saturday they would mow the lawn or rake the leaves and then play ball (or dolls). On Sunday they went to church, had a great dinner, and then played catch with dad or played games with neighbors or cousins.

Holidays were a big deal back then. Thanksgiving, Christmas, New Year's Day, Memorial Day and Labor Day all called for the cousins to get together at grandma and grandpa's for a feast and party. These were wonderful get-togethers with great food followed by fun games. The grown-ups would play cards and the kids would play board games (when it was cold outside) or go outside and play games. Those holiday get-togethers helped define a family. Your first cousins were often your best friends.

Today it is hard to even define a family. Men are marrying men and women are marrying women. Kids are no longer considered a gift but rather a responsibility or worse, a burden. In the traditional man-woman marriage arrangement, both normally work outside of the home. This often isn't due to the need to provide the basics for the family, but rather to provide a second or third car, a bigger house, a second house, etc. Jobs take precedence over faith and family. The kids have a nanny stay with them after school, or go to a relative's house until one of the parents comes by with fast food in order to pick them up and take them home or, more likely, to take them to practice. If one of the parents does not have a job outside the house, he or she becomes an Uber driver for the kids. All have the required SUV, and all put many miles on that SUV toting the kids to every kind of practice you can imagine. Family evening dinner consists of opening the sacks of fast food and distributing it among those kids who are around. It is a rare day when mom or dad cooks a meal and all of the family is home to enjoy family dinner (6 PM). Homework, if there is any, is done on a laptop or an iPad, and the parents can't tell if their kids are doing homework, texting friends, or surfing the Internet. Children no longer go out and play after school or after supper (if they don't have X-ball practice). Instead they quickly retire to their room to get on their smart phone and spend the rest of the evening communicating electronically with only who knows who. The whole family thing has turned into a disaster.

Sundays are no longer a day of rest. Church has given way to false idols - soccer (name the sport) is now the lord of Sundays for the kids and one parent (the SUV driver), and the god of golf takes up Sunday morning/afternoon for dads.

Most kids now go to college, even if they shouldn't. If they graduate, they take a job (hopefully) but it is usually someplace a distance away from home. If they don't graduate (or sometimes even when they do graduate), they move back into their parents' basement.

Holidays are no longer spent at grandma and grandpa's, since no one lives close enough anymore. Plus going to grandma and grandpa's is boring.

Of all the things that have changed over my years on the planet, I believe that the family has taken the biggest hit (with faith being a close second). Our nuclear family has been abused and continues to be destroyed. And that is really sad to me. The family is the building block of society. Without a strong family, our country will not survive.

So what is the solution? Faith. We must restore God to his proper place. First of all, Sunday is His. He gave us the Sabbath to spend time worshiping him and resting. We as a nation need to do that. Return to going to church on Sunday (Saturday for those who celebrate it as their Sabbath). Do your shopping and other chores on Saturday, and make Sunday "God and Family Day" with your God, your kids and your extended family.

Second, make every effort possible to share a family dinner at home every weekday. Gather around the table and share your day's ups and downs. Ban any smartphones, TV's, etc. This is family time – period.

Third, start or restart family traditions. Go to grandma and grandpa's for a holiday or two. Tell stories with the kids there about your times growing up. Share your family's heritage and install a sense of pride in your family name.

Lastly, stop working yourself to the bone pursuing the American dream. If you have a family, you already possess the American dream! You don't need a better SUV, house, vacation home, etc. to be happy. Believe me, when you get as old as I am, you will look back and treasure the times you spent with your family – you won't look back on that red sports car and think "Wow, that was so worth giving up everything else so that I could be seen driving that car."

So what are my takeaways from this experience?

1. *Reestablish family relationships and traditions if you truly want to be happy.*

Chapter 15 – Faith

Geez, where do I start with this one? As I said in the family chapter, the two areas that have taken the biggest hits in my lifetime are family and faith. As I was growing up people were never ashamed of their faith. You assumed that everyone had it (even if the Protestants were considered second class heavenly citizens according to a few nuns that taught in our Catholic grade school).

I had mentioned blue laws in an earlier chapter. To remind you, in case you forgot what blue laws were, they prohibited businesses, except for emergency services, from being open on Sunday. These laws, based on God's word, made sure you had every opportunity to worship and rest on Sunday. This made worship much easier than it is today. Almost everyone attended church services every Sunday morning and no one worked. Think of that - we as a country (most cities and states) held praising God as so important that we passed civil laws to help make that happen. No one in government said you had to go to church, or be a Jew or a Baptist - you were free to worship your God wherever you chose. The government simply made it easier to do so.

Back then prayer was simply a part of everyday life. Kids prayed in school, regardless if it was a parochial or public school. What we learned at home and at church was reinforced at school - God and prayer were integral parts of our daily lives.

Back then it was not unusual to see individuals and families pray before a meal in public.

The only downside I can recall is the misleading guidance we got from a very few nuns at our grade school back then. They told us not to be-friend non-Catholics, and to not attend a non-Catholic Church service. I can understand where they were coming from, since God instructed the Israelites not to marry or interact with non-Jews. God told them that this would lead to the Jewish people eventually worshiping the false gods of the non-Jews.

However, almost every, if not every, non-Catholic I knew was a Christian. We believed in the same God and these were good people. (For goodness sake, we share the first 1500 years of church history together.) Looking back, I wish those few nuns would have approached this differently. I do understand the difficulty a family can encounter when the husband and wife are from different denominations. This is not only difficult but also confusing for the children when witnessing their parents attending different church services. Obviously it is so much better when both parents attend the same church service and have similar belief systems. But judging others to be less than us spiritually because of the church service they attend is not right. God knows each of our hearts – let us leave it up to Him to decide how much a person's soul pleases Him.

Looking at faith in America today makes me sad. Our government has done a 180 degree turn on us. Instead of blue laws, now we have laws that prohibit prayer in school and some public places. Our government not only fails to protect the most vulnerable lives there are in the world, they actually support and encourage killing unborn babies and want all Americans to pay for this abomination. Our government persecutes people of faith who refuse to participate in acts that go against their religious beliefs (for example, baking and selling a wedding cake for a gay couple, forcing religious organizations to provide contraceptives and abortion services as part of their health care plans, etc.).

Anti-religious groups are getting the support of government at all levels. Manger scenes are being forced to be removed from public property, as are crosses. People are being arrested for praying outside of abortion clinics. Our government has become atheistic.

I talked about this in a previous chapter, but I have to mention again just how devastating the entertainment industry has been to the faith and lifestyles of Americans, especially young people. Movies, TV, music, advertising, the Internet - you name it, all have infiltrated the minds of the public with ego-driven materialism, violence, pornography and the like. People are bombarded daily with evil. It is non-stop, and you are seeing the results of our leaving God by the numbers of violent crimes, suicides, rapes, abortions, thefts, burglaries, divorces, etc., in the US today.

Ethical behavior, once a stalwart of America, is now seldom found. Unethical behavior has permeated the federal, state and local governments as well as the media. You need to go no further than the Russian hoax that was played out during Donald Trump's four years in office. It was all based on lies, and it took multitudes within government and the media to mislead the American public for over 4 years. What's even worse from an ethical standpoint is that none of these liars will probably ever have to serve time in jail for their unethical behavior.

From a positive standpoint, what all this evil in today's world has done for faith is that it has crystallized it. There are fewer people of faith today, in my opinion, but their faith is very strong. They are what I believe the Bible calls "the remnant." It also has caused people to have to choose between right and wrong, God and the evil one. We have come to a point where you have to pick sides. The government and media have forced this on us. We must choose to be vaccinated or not, we must choose to be patriotic or not, we must choose to choose abortion or not, and we must choose to be Christian or not.

So what's the solution to the problems of restoring faith in God to America? I think there are only two things that can restore faith in America: prayer and love. We're at a point in our country where man's solutions will not work. We're at a point where only God can rectify our situation. As our Blessed Mother has been saying in Medjugorje, Croatia for 40 years - pray, pray, pray. We must pray for the conversion of our leaders as well as our neighbors and ourselves. (As a good friend says, "We all killed Christ.") Every day. Pray. Pray. Pray.

Love will certainly be required for us to continue to pray for the conversion of America (and the world). It is so much easier to hate than to love. We must show others Jesus' love by our actions. Kindness, compassion and caring will show others what faith in God is and what it is all about. I'm not talking about being a wimp - we still must stand up for what is right, just and good. But we need to do it without malice or hate. We must do it with love in our heart, kindness in our eyes, and courage in our spirit. We can be both strong and meek. (Meekness being whereby a person is willing to accept and submit without resistance to the will and desire of God.) God will not forsake us if we trust in Him.

So what is my takeaway from this experience?

1. *Without praying for the conversion of America (and the world), our American way of life is history.* We have become a divided nation because we have pushed God out of our lives. We need to replace hate and division with love and prayer. We must remember we are all brethren.

Chapter 16 – Environment

The big thing growing up in the 50's was litter. People often simply threw trash out of their car window when they were done eating, drinking or smoking something. If you drove down a highway, you saw quite a bit of litter along the sides of the road. I don't know if it was purposeful or just a coincidence, but as the federal government was completing the interstate highway system, a huge push was put on by all governmental jurisdictions to clean up the litter. Laws were enacted that made it illegal to litter. If caught, you could be fined $100 or more, which was a lot of money back then. (My mom was working at a dry cleaner making 90 cents per hour at the time.)

Another big environmental issue was smog in big cities and industrial towns. Emissions from automobiles and industry polluted the air. In my hometown of Lima, Ohio, you could see the haze when looking south. Autos, trucks and other motorized equipment could possibly be a problem everywhere, but our town, being a regional industrial center with many factories, did have some air quality issues. The worst polluters, I believe, were the oil refineries. There were numerous large refineries in south Lima, and the emissions coming from them caused the sky to often look yellow.

Beyond the 50's and 60's, water quality and air quality issues led President Richard Nixon in December of 1970 to form the Environmental Protection Agency (EPA). New laws were passed by Congress to protect our air (1970 Clean Air Act), water (1972 Clean Water Act), and our wetlands (precursor to 1986 Wetlands Protection Act was passed in 1977). The EPA was formed to enforce these laws.

Nuclear waste from nuclear power plants was the big issue in the 80's, and is more than likely the reason that nuclear power plants were no longer built after 1996. (A new reactor did come on line in 2016 and two more are currently being built in Georgia.)

Global warming first became a concern to some scientists in the 80's, but many other scientists even today feel that the earth is in an interglacial period (a geological interval of warmer global average temperature lasting thousands of years) that separates consecutive glacial periods within an ice age.

For us, if you did not live in a big city with a lot of auto traffic or in an industrial town, you never noticed any air pollution. Likewise, streams were still clean, unless they were located near industries that polluted them with waste from their factories. Our big concern growing up was all that litter that was strewn along the highways. It took a number of years, but eventually most Americans' habits changed and they pretty much stopped littering. The Clean Air, Water and Wetlands Acts followed the same pattern. It took a while for them to make a big difference, but eventually they did. Manufacturers changed the way they made gas engines and close scrutiny of what was going into our streams made our air and water much cleaner.

All in all, the environmental issues of the 50's and 60's were pretty well cleaned up by the late 70's and early 80's.

[As a side note, plastic was not the problem it is today as far as waste disposal was concerned. Until about 1982, bags used by grocers and other retail stores were paper bags. Clerks would place peoples' groceries into paper bags. When the customer got home, they did not throw the bag away. They used it to line the kitchen trash can. Among other things, they used it also as book covers for school books that the school loaned to students - back then, you did not have to buy your books. They recycled them from year to year. Therefore, you put a paper bag cover on them on which you could write practically anything. You never wrote in your school book. If you didn't take care of it, you paid a fine at the end of the school year.]

Today global warming has dominated the environmental issues for not only the U.S., but also much of the rest of the world. This issue had been classified as global cooling in the 70's and 80's due to the fact that from 1940 to about 1975 the average global surface temperature decreased by about 0.1 degrees Celsius, interrupting a decades-long warming. When the global cooling fanatics finally saw data that indicated the planet was warming again, they changed their tune and screamed about global warming being the thing that will end our way of life. When pushback came from some scientists challenging their theories, they changed the "global warming" language to "climate change." Now that is all you hear. Everything is caused by "climate change."

Here is my take on it – our planet has climate cycles. Some cycles will cool the earth for a period of time, and some will warm it. I think it is somewhat arrogant of humans to think we can predict what is going to happen weather-wise in the future. Do we really believe that because we drive gas combustion engine cars and cows have flatulence that we are having more hurricanes, blizzards, droughts, forest fires, etc.? According to the Heartland Institute, a free-market think tank based in Illinois, "The number of tornadoes has been declining for the past 50 years, and the number of strong tornadoes, F3 or higher, has dramatically declined (from about 60/year to 20/year) over the past 50 years." You will never hear that statistic from the mainstream media, who push climate change narratives constantly. This world has been around for quite some time and to think we humans can control climate and weather is vanity. There are things we can do to help keep our planet clean and beautiful, and we must make every effort to do just that. Polluting our streams, rivers and oceans is wrong. Controlling air pollutants should be a goal of ours, and protecting natural habitats is our duty. But eliminating clean coal, natural gas, and some other fossil fuels is not the answer. Why are we not using nuclear energy to replace dirty coal instead of eliminating clean coal entirely? Nuclear waste control is not an issue. (In a 2018 Forbes article written by Michael Shellenberger concerning nuclear waste, he states, "How much is there? If all the nuclear waste from U.S. power plants were put on a football field, it would stack up just 50 feet high. In comparison to the waste produced by every other kind of electricity production, that quantity is close to zero.") Also, the safety of nuclear plants has improved. The last nuclear accident was in Japan in 2011. And with better technological controls, we can limit the occurrences from the current one every 10 to 20 years to something much longer.

Engine technology has improved significantly over the years, and the introduction of battery driven cars has been a great improvement environmentally. (Electric cars are still a big question mark for me – what are we going to use to re-charge these vehicles? If you eliminate fossil fuels and nuclear energy, where do you get the "juice" to re-charge your car? Don't tell me wind – that is pretty much a big loser when it comes to generating energy, and solar energy still needs significant improvement to generate enough energy to make a difference.)

Bottom line on the difference in the environment "back when" and now is that our problems in my day were not as hard to tackle, and were not as politically charged as today's issues. When we lived on the farm we never even thought about the air not being clean. The creek's water was muddy, but also unpolluted, so we never thought about not being able to eat the catfish we caught in it. Litter along the highway was an issue, but litter wasn't a problem away from the highway. You wouldn't think of throwing out even a gum wrapper on your neighbors' property. At home the water that was used came from an unpolluted well located normally next to the house. Many homes were heated by propane, so that was not an environmental issue. We weren't even aware of air pollution from automobiles, because normally you didn't drive your car during the week if you were working on the farm. When you did drive, you only drove into town, which was about five miles away. You did use a gas engine tractor, but no one considered that to cause atmospheric issues because there just weren't many tractors burning fuel compared to the number of cars on the road. Life was much simpler, and politics did not seem to interfere with your life environmentally.

Today, politics, especially on the national and global level, drive the environmental movement. We are told that "Climate Change" has become the reason for most evils in the world. This propaganda is currently responsible for major changes in the way we live in the U.S. "The Green New Deal" is being pushed to change what and how we drive, eat, manufacture, heat and cool our homes and offices, etc. The goal of the plan is to bring U.S. greenhouse gas emissions down to net-zero while meeting 100% of power demand in the country through clean, renewable, and zero-emission energy sources. Those sources are primarily solar and wind power. Unfortunately, in my opinion, technology has not provided the means of getting enough solar power without covering our entire country with solar panels. And wind power is pretty much a joke. Without government subsidies to the electric utilities, wind power would not be used at all in today's grid. Studies have been done that show the wind must <u>average</u> over 25 miles per hour for a wind turbine to financially produce more energy than it costs to produce it. There are few places in the world where the wind averages 25 miles per hour. Until technology brings down that number, wind turbines are a big loser, both financially and aesthetically. Personally I would love to see the power of the sun and wind harnessed – but I do not want to be lied to by politicians who claim sun and wind power can and must replace our current energy production (nuclear, clean coal, natural gas, and petroleum).

Unlike the days past, politics has reared its ugly head when it comes to the environment. Gone are the days of substantiated facts used to resolve issues and create solutions. Now it is all about "spinning" data to support your respective agenda. Sadly, I don't believe that will change in my lifetime.

So what are my takeaways from this experience?

1. *Renewable energy sources need to be further researched and developed.* Harnessing sun and wind energy is a noble goal and should be pursued vigorously. However, trying to make a flash cut to these sources and eliminating fossil fuels is ludicrous today. We as a nation are not ready to make that leap. We should continue to use clean coal, natural gas and nuclear power to provide most of our energy needs, while continuing to find better ways to generate sun and wind energy. I believe that technology would allow us to make a slow, gradual move to renewable energy sources that would be efficient and effective. But the technology is not there yet, so don't force it on the nation until it makes economic sense.
2. *Plastic needs to be controlled.* We use plastic for everything today. That is both good and bad. Plastic has allowed us to make many things that are lighter, more durable, and less expensive than other materials used in the past. However, we must get a handle on discarding it. We can't keep polluting our oceans and filling our land fills with it. We have to get everyone to buy in to recycling plastic and reduce the production of items created with new plastic. Again, technology and discipline both play a big role in accomplishing this.

Chapter 17 – Mass Media

Growing up I didn't watch the TV news all that much, although I was aware that the main networks had a nightly news show right around supper time. The only one I remember listening to was Walter Cronkite on the CBS Evening News. I remember believing what Cronkite would tell me on the evening news program. For some reason I trusted him. Later I read that Cronkite refused to allow his personal beliefs to affect his job of reporting accurate news. It was his integrity and commitment to fair reporting which established him as "the most trusted man in America." David Brinkley was on NBC, but he just wasn't as likable as Walter Cronkite was. I'm sure he was as trustworthy, because back then you were a journalist first and kept your opinions to yourself. To be honest, I don't know who ABC had as their news anchor.

Local news was local news. They simply reported what was going on in the neighborhood. There are still some of those broadcast news outlets today, although they too are becoming scarcer.

Newspapers and magazines were more slanted on their reporting than the national broadcast networks were, in my opinion. (We just found out in the last few years how the New York Times failed to report the atrocities the Jews in Europe were experiencing during World War II.) An article I read from the Hoover Institute said that the media (newspapers mainly) were biased as far back as the 19th century. Editors slanted the news based on their opinion of what would be good for the country, influencing "citizens who needed guiding by their betters in order to understand and choose the policies necessary for improving society." Although this goes against the grain for many citizens, the good news was that there were so many newspapers with so many different opinions that they somewhat balanced each other out.

This began to change drastically in the 70's when broadcast media took off and many newspapers went out of business. With fewer newspapers, there were fewer opinions being reported, and thus the main reporting entities had a much greater influence on citizens. Simultaneously, the industry's labor force changed. Prior to this, according to the Hoover Institution article, "newspapermen" were people who did not have journalism degrees but rather were people who worked their way up the ladder to become reporters. Therefore their bias was not ideological but rather based on the class they came from. In the 70's journalism became a profession that was certified by a university degree. It was at this point that the liberal bent of universities began their huge influence on how and what their graduates reported. You see today the result of this phenomenon. Mainstream Media is significantly biased toward liberal ideology.

Although the scale is heavily weighted toward liberal reporting today, there was a ray of hope that was introduced in the 90's when cable networks and the internet came online. They allowed opposing views to be opined, and it kept the public from being swamped with only one side of the story. This rivalry became fierce in the 21st century with the rise of Obama and Trump. This rivalry was healthy, in my opinion, for it gave people alternative views on things that were going on in the country and the world. However, during President Trump's time in office, things changed drastically. High tech, government and media joined forces to limit or eliminate opposing views to the liberal agenda. People who shared opinions or even facts that differed from the liberal narrative were censored. This, again in my opinion, was a direct violation of the First Amendment to the Constitution. Those in power were controlling what we as citizens could say or hear. I don't believe the American general public realizes what a great threat this is to our democracy itself. If you go back and look at Germany before World War II, you will see many similarities to today's United States. People went along with the government's intrusion as long as it didn't directly affect them. By not standing up and fighting the wrongs that were being done to fellow Germans, the remainder of the population eventually became "subjects" of the German Nazi government. You did it their way, or else you were off to the concentration camps. And their media went right along with the government's narrative.

We are facing many of these same intrusions today in the U.S. The Covid-19 pandemic gave government an opportunity to take away our right to live free and make our own personal decisions. It started with the mandates and lock-downs that were supposed to last two weeks in order to "flatten the curve." Here we are, over two years later, and nothing has changed. Many states, schools and businesses require you to wear a mask even if you have had Covid or have received the so called "vaccines." Now they are finding out that masks do not prevent the airborne virus (especially the Omicron strain) from entering your system, which is what quite a few doctors said back two years ago. Those doctors were censored by Big Tech and the Media. School children, in particular, were forced to wear masks the entire school day, even though they are minutely at risk of getting Covid or transmitting the virus to others. Parents had no say in the matter. Now in some jurisdictions this "dictatorship" mentality is moving into the area of giving children "the Jab" without the knowledge of the parent. This isn't only wrong; this is evil in my opinion. In addition, some jurisdictions are requiring proof of "vaccination" before you can participate in public events. New York is probably the worst of all the states, especially New York City. Now getting the "vaccinations" and boosters do not prevent you from contracting Covid or transmitting it to others, but these government leaders don't care – they require their citizens to get the shots anyway or else be isolated and chastised as the "unvaccinated." This entire narrative is strongly supported by the media, with a few cable TV channels and some Internet websites presenting the "other side" of the science and the argument. The federal government, Big Tech and the media are doing everything possible to silence these sources so that the American public does not have access to alternative facts and opinions.

Over the last two years, common sense has left the planet! It is time for Americans to stand up for common sense. If we don't, we will become just like Germany and Italy of the 40's. We can't sit on our hands and wait for someone else to take the lead on this. Each one of us, in our own personal way, must have the courage to fight these principles and policies. We must speak up. We must act. Time is of the essence. We must have the courage of our forefathers who fought the Nazi's in WWII. We can't let tyranny continue to rule in the U.S.

So what are my takeaways from this experience?

1. *Mass Media has to return to the role of watchdog.*

So what can be done as it concerns the Media and their partnership with the federal government? First, we should talk with our pocketbook. (Some of these may be difficult to do for many of us.)

- Cancel subscriptions to media outlets and print media who fail to share all the facts with us.
- Stop going to retailers who push the narrative and instead frequent retailers who stay out of politics.
- Stop using online services like Google, Twitter, Facebook and YouTube who use their monopoly power to control what is and is not presented on their platforms and start using alternative sources.
- Write letters to the editors that voice your strong disapproval of how they cover the news of the day.

Chapter 18 – Government

I must admit that growing up I did not pay much attention to government at any level. I heard my dad say he was a Republican, but I didn't know what that meant. Ohio was apparently more Republican than Democrat, but back then there didn't seem to be much difference between the two. The main differences centered on their economic policies.

The 1952 presidential platforms somewhat mirrored each other. The Republicans wanted to end the war in Korea, limit the power of labor unions, opposed discrimination based on race, color or creed, develop nuclear weapons as a deterrent, and end communist subversion in the U.S. The Democrats also favored a strong national defense, collective security against the Soviet Union, equal employment opportunities for minorities and continued efforts to fight racial discrimination. They differed from the Republicans in that they wanted to fund public assistance for the aged, children, the blind and disabled; expansion of the school lunch program; and expanding the power of labor unions. So you can see that there really wasn't much difference between the two parties. In fact, I once read that both parties courted General Dwight D. Eisenhower to be their presidential candidate. "Ike" chose the Republicans, and won the 1952 and 1956 presidential elections.

Again, my how things have changed. Today these two parties are polar opposites. The Republicans push conservative principles, and the Democrats push liberal policies. At the national level, there are extremely few things these two parties agree upon. This divide has trickled down to the state and local levels. There are still some independents out there, but if you are a Republican or a Democrat, you are pretty much hard core. Government empowerment, abortion, economic policy, foreign relations policy, immigration, taxing policy, energy policy and welfare are areas in which the two parties line up on opposite sides. Whichever party is in power shoves their ideology down the other's throat. Working together for the overall good of the country is non-existent. This really baffles me, for there are things that could be agreed upon and implemented to improve our country.

Immigration is one that has been a low hanging fruit for years. Most Americans want a sovereign border and an orderly and legal method of allowing immigrants to enter our country and be given the opportunity to become citizens. So why is our southern border like a sieve? My opinion is that liberals think those crossing illegally will eventually be able to vote, and vote Democrat, and Republican business owners want cheap labor that is available by hiring illegal aliens. The normal American simply wants a process to be in place that allows an orderly infusion of people from other countries who will help America grow and become a better country. That is how we became who we are – immigrants from all over the world came to America, followed the process of gaining citizenry, established communities in the U.S. that produced workers, small businesses, and new traditions while assimilating into the American culture. How hard is it for our political leaders to reestablish this process? Most laws are already on the books – we simply need to enforce them and tweak the ones that can be improved.

The other major difference between the two parties is the idea that the government is the solution to all of our problems versus getting the government out of our lives and letting us solve our own problems. I really struggle to find something that the government does that is actually more efficient and effective than what can be done privately. Our government was originally established to keep us safe and free. Creating an army that will defend us, establishing laws that treat all Americans fairly, regulating interstate commerce, and enforcing those laws are plenty for a national government to do. We don't need them interfering with state or local jurisdictions where the local citizens know what is best for themselves. I am utterly amazed at just how wise our founding fathers were when they developed our federal republic. The sharing of power between the national government and the state governments was ingenious, as was the "checks and balances" provided by the three branches of government – the executive, the legislative and the judicial. Unfortunately, in many cases, power-hungry politicians have politicized all three branches and blurred the lines for proper checks and balances. Plus, since the Civil War the power of the federal government has expanded greatly. Personally I don't believe that was what our founding fathers intended to happen. Today, the federal government tries to run our lives. They do not recognize that the way things are done in New York or California is not the same way things are done in Texas or South Dakota. One size does not fit all, which has been exemplified strongly with the government's response to the coronavirus pandemic. Interestingly, the states that developed their own processes for fighting the virus while keeping the economy going have fared much better than those who followed the federal government's dictates and lock downs (e.g., Florida vs. California or New York). The power-grab that has been on display since the virus hit is wrong and very concerning.

What is driving the collapse of our way of governing? Money. Greed. Power. In today's political process, normally whoever has the most money wins the elected position in a contested jurisdiction. Freeing up people and corporations to fund Political Action Committees (PAC) without limits is destroying our elective process. It blows your mind when you see how many tens of millions of dollars are spent on a single congressional campaign, or the hundreds of millions of dollars spent on a single senatorial campaign. Because of this obscene spending, normal everyday citizens can't be candidates any longer. You have to be either extremely wealthy or sell your soul to various lobbying groups, or both. In a majority of cases our elected officials owe their position to a PAC or a lobbying group and find themselves compromised when having to vote on a bill that goes against these groups' desires. In my opinion, the only way to stop this insanity is to stop the flow of money to campaigns. I would favor having each campaign equally funded by our government at a reasonably modest set amount per elected position, and then eliminating all other funding, including in-kind contributions. Put everyone on a level playing field, and allow your next door neighbor to run for office if he/she so desires. Unfortunately, like term limits, this will never happen. There is too much money and power at stake, and we don't have leaders who have the integrity or fortitude to make this happen.

So what are my takeaways from this experience?

1. *I don't believe that the status quo will change without a drastic collapse of the economy.* War won't do it. Common sense won't do it. Preaching the faith won't do it. Only financial collapse will get the attention of all of America. If and when this happens, and provided Americans can still have a fair election, Americans will finally see the federal government for what it really is, i.e., an enormous organization that uses tax payer funds to make themselves powerful, controlling and wealthy. Call it the "Deep State" or whatever name you want to give it – there is a permanent class of federal employees (elected and non-elected) who will not allow change to happen that will jeopardize their positions. Only an economic collapse whereby additional money cannot be printed, forcing government to have to be severely reduced, will open the door to governmental reform and a return to the original purpose of a federal government – i.e., providing safety and protecting freedom.

Chapter 19 – Freedom

I saved this for last, because it is probably the hardest one to write about. I should probably start with a definition of freedom, or at least define what freedom is not. Freedom is not doing whatever you want, whenever you want, with or to whoever you want. That is anarchy.

Here are a few quotes from famous people as to what they think freedom is:

- "May we think of freedom, not as the right to do as we please, but as the opportunity to do what is right." Peter Marshall
- "Freedom consists not in doing what we like, but in having the right to do what we ought." Pope John Paul II
- "My definition of a free society is a society where it is safe to be unpopular." Adlai Stevenson
- "Nothing is more difficult, and therefore more precious than to be able to decide." Napoleon Bonaparte
- "A man who believes in freedom will do anything under the sun to acquire, or preserve his freedom." Malcolm X

If I can glean a few items from the above quotes, I'd zero in on:

- Opportunity to do what is right (what we ought to do)
- Safe to be unpopular
- Being able to decide
- Worth fighting for

These items show freedom as the ability to decide freely, to choose the right thing even if our opinion is unpopular, and to defend those rights at all costs.

We were so blessed to have been born in (or legally migrated to) America. I just shake my head at how wise our founding fathers were when they designed our government. I had mentioned this in the previous chapter, but it is worth repeating - three separate but co-equal branches of government that are charged with doing what is right for the people but does not infringe upon the rights of the states who make up the country – wow! When creating our nation these men had to negotiate such a fine line and sensitive balance. Only God's help, in my opinion, could have guided them to come to such an agreement for the new country. They based their design on Christian values and ended up with the closest thing to freedom that had ever been established by men to rule each other. The Framers decided to create a limited government based on the ideas of natural rights, popular sovereignty, republicanism, and the social contract (the Constitution).

Limited government is a political system in which there are certain restrictions placed on the government to protect individual rights and liberties. This decision to create a limited government was a deliberate departure from the British monarchy, which the Framers felt violated their rights. They intentionally created a limited government that would have to abide by a set of rules designed by the people of the country. So what are the 3 main purposes of a limited US government?

- Maintain social order
- Provide some public services
- Provide security and defense

That is it. You can argue as to the extent of the definitions of social order, public services, security and defense, but there are so many things that our government has decided to benevolently provide today that it has caused all three of these purposes to have become significantly blurred.

Growing up in America in the 50's, we had much more emphasis on local and state jurisdiction than federal jurisdiction. The local government provided police, fire, and legal services to administer the social order. The state provided the highway patrol for U.S. highways, state law representation, and commerce regulations. The federal government provided the FBI and interstate commerce regulations. The lines between these jurisdictions were pretty well defined. The feds did not impose upon the states, and the states did not impose upon the locals, as a general rule.

As far as public services were concerned, again the smaller jurisdictions provided the most. Water, gas & electricity, etc. were guided by local ordinances under some state guidelines. Telephone service was under state regulation. Road maintenance was both local and state, and later on when the interstate highway system was developed, the feds got more involved. Welfare did not exist. The closest thing to it was social security, but that was funded by the individual and his employer and the federal government was to simply act as the administrator. Most services that were provided, such as medical, dental, etc., were private but under state regulations. Things were pretty simple back then.

The federal government's main job was to keep the country safe. A military made up of citizens from all 48 states was funded by the citizens of all 48 states, and the task of keeping us secure and defended was the job of the federal government under the direction of the Commander-in-Chief, the President.

Once again, there has been a drastic change in who does what and what all is considered social order, public services and safety & defense. We are now extremely top heavy, with the federal government intruding into our lives with everything from mandated health care to how much water our shower head is allowed to provide. Over the last 50 plus years there has been a power grab at the federal level. I attribute that mainly to technology and the notion of providing greater security. Communication has become instantaneous, and everyone seems to know everyone else's business. We have developed a political system that empowers certain "elites" to determine what is good for all the people. It doesn't matter if you live in New York, Alabama, Kansas, North Dakota, New Mexico or California – whatever Washington D.C. thinks is best for you is best for you!

I think back to the days of living on the farm with Grandma and Grandpa. Grandpa kept a shot gun and a rifle in the coat closet in the kitchen. He did not have to have a license to own the guns. He did not have to take any training course to be able to use the gun – his dad taught him how to do that. He was expected to be responsible for how the guns were used and by whom. Not so today. We have to register every gun that is purchased and undergo a background check before the sale is authorized. We are told by our federal government that guns need to be controlled, since so many people are killed by guns each year. No, guns don't kill people, people kill people. You wonder why there are so many murders now versus when I grew up? Simple answer – it has little to do with the availability of more guns and everything to do with our nation no longer having a moral compass. When we took prayer out of the schools in the early 60's and have been taking God out of the fabric of our nation ever since, it is quite obvious why behaviors have changed. Who is teaching right from wrong these days? It sure isn't happening in the schools, and with the "hippie" generation now in charge of everything, anything goes. Those free love folks of the Woodstock generation have raised a generation of children with no moral compass, who now themselves are raising a second generation of similar valueless children. Divorce and abortion have skyrocketed, so why wouldn't murders also?

We now have a society that is out of control. In order to try to control this harmful behavior, more and more laws have been and are being passed, especially at the federal level. More and more federal regulations are being implemented in an attempt to control the behavior of the citizens. Corruption has infiltrated all of our institutions, including not only our government, but also our businesses, churches and schools. You can hardly trust anyone in a leadership position anymore. All seem to have a hidden agenda from which they will personally benefit.

What all of this quagmire has done is to put more and more restrictions on our lives. We are losing our freedom. We are being told that we have to have health insurance or we will be fined; we must take an experimental gene therapy "jab" or we can't participate in normal societal activities and events; we are forced to wear masks, even though it has been proven that masks do not prevent the contracting or the spread of the coronavirus; we are being forced to give up fossil fuel produced energy in the name of "climate change;" we are being forced to accept millions of illegal aliens and then fund them once they are in our country in the name of compassion; we are being forced to fund wars that have no significant benefit for our country, again in the name of compassion. The list goes on and on. Our country today is so far from what it was after World War II that it has become unrecognizable. We are on the brink of losing the greatest country to have ever been established on the planet earth.

In my opinion, our future as a free citizen in a free country is dismal. We have a federal government in place that not only wants to control our behavior; they also want to dictate what that behavior should be. I am not only talking about elected officials – I am including the whole bureaucracy. To me, it is obvious that both political parties are in on it, and have been for a long time. Proof of that is as simple as to look back on what happened when a political outsider (Donald Trump) became President and tried to do things that benefited the common man. A firestorm of resistance was immediately ignited and continued for his entire term. People within the government lied and cheated and did things for which they should have been tried and put in prison – but none were held accountable by any federal legislative body or government law enforcement organization. And don't think that electing Republicans in the 2022 mid-term elections will make a difference. We will continue to see those conservatives who are elected and who believe in limited government and personal freedom ostracized by those elected officials who are either currently in place and are re-elected or not up for re-election. I personally do not think the tide can be turned – we are too far down the road and too many of our federal officials are owned by special interest groups and lobbyists or foreign countries. Just look around – do you know anyone who was elected to the House or the Senate who did not become wealthy during or after they completed their terms?

Bottom line for me is that the only thing that can cause our future to change for the better is what I mentioned in an earlier chapter – a total financial collapse of the country. That is sad, but without everything being wiped out, America cannot or will not start over.

I am sure that many of you reading this think dementia or Alzheimer's has set in, seeing I am 70+. But no, that is not the case. I am simply looking at history, both world and biblical history, to analyze what has gone before us. In ancient history Rome is a great example of how internal corruption led to its downfall. In more recent history the same happened to Germany, Italy and Russia. In biblical history it is hard to count how many times the Israelites had established a strong nation only to be wiped out by neighboring nations due to their failure to follow God's laws. Why do you think it will be any different for America?

So what are my takeaways from this experience?

1. *The "good old days" of the 50's and 60's really were the "good old days" from a freedom perspective*. Since then, the federal government has gained considerable power over our daily lives and our freedom has been significantly diminished. That is not going to change. All we can do is pray that God blesses us and changes hearts, and be a strong beacon for the truth when it is time for us to stand up and courageously voice that truth.

Chapter 20 – Summary Analysis

Chances are you are a little depressed after reading parts of this book. It seems like we are headed in the wrong direction in so many areas of our lives. Before making a final judgement though, let's review the chapters and what we gleaned from each so that we can get an overall picture of life in the 50's and 60's versus life today in America.

To do that, I have created a table that lists the pros and cons of each chapter. After reviewing the table, we'll make an overall assessment of the state of the Union.

Analysis Table

Chap	Topic	50's & 60's	Today	Better or Worse Today
1	The Way We Were	Sacrifice, discipline, prayer & trust in God spells success	What's in it for me?	Worse
2	Simple Times, Simple Formula	Formula for happiness and peace = six days of work and one day of rest	Every day is just like the previous/next day	Worse
3	The Three R's	Learned the fundamentals which became the building blocks	Use technology to do the basics & incorporate ideology into the curriculum	Worse
4	Advanced Education	College was limited to those who could afford it. Practical skills taught in high school for non-college track students.	College available to practically everyone, but practical skills very limited	Neutral
5	Jobs & Careers	Jobs were hard. Careers were meaningful. Employee/Employer relationship healthy.	Jobs more interesting. Careers more challenging. Employer/employee relationship based on skill value.	Neutral

Chap	Topic	50's & 60's	Today	Better or Worse Today
6	Money	Credit was non-existent, so you only bought what you could afford.	Credit has gone berserk, both for the individual and for the government. Economic disaster is on the horizon.	Worse
7	Shopping	In-store shopping dominated.	Online shopping and big box stores dominate.	Better
8	Entertainmt	Content was family oriented. Technology was primitive.	Content has no limits. Technology is terrific.	Neutral
9	Comedy	Great content. Gifted comedians.	Bad content. Comedic hacks.	Worse
10	Travel	Poor roads and limited flight choices. Time consuming to travel.	Jet Service and Interstate highways create easy travel options.	Better
11	Exercise & Health	Ate nutritiously. Exercise was part of work.	Bad food & drink. Limited exercise, even though it is more available.	Worse
12	Healthcare	Patient oriented. Not too expensive.	Huge gain due to technology, but gov't intrusion has jettisoned prices.	Better
13	Race Relations	Open prejudice and segregation.	Freedom & opportunities for all to succeed.	Better

Chap	Topic	50's & 60's	Today	Better or Worse Today
14	Family	Took priority over all other things except maybe church.	Broken and fragmented. Second class citizen.	Worse
15	Faith	Sundays belonged to God.	We are turning into an atheistic nation.	Worse
16	Environment	Air quality in big cities and litter along highways were issues.	"Climate Change" now dominates the headlines. Attempting to eliminate fossil fuel.	Better
17	Mass Media	Journalists were not "opinion-ists." News could be trusted.	Everything is subject to a "spin" when reported on by the media.	Worse
18	Government	Political parties' ideology rather similar.	Political parties' ideology polar opposites. Fed Gov't expansion a threat to individual's freedom.	Worse
19	Freedom	Limited fed gov't. Stronger state and local govt's.	Greatly expanded Fed Gov't. Loss of freedom for the individual.	Worse

Being a competitive type of person, I naturally peruse the far right column and keep track of the "score." I come up with "today" being:

- better off - 5 categories
- neutral   - 3 categories
- worse off - 11 categories

Chapter 21 – Conclusion

The results of the Analysis Chart above do not surprise me. Looking at it from strictly a mathematical perspective, we are certainly worse off today than we were when I was growing up. However, you can't just look at this from a mathematical perspective. Some categories should be weighed more heavily than others should, because they are more important to society as a whole. I, personally put more emphasis on the following categories: Faith, Family, Freedom, Education and then Government, Exercise & Health, and Mass Media, in that order.

I put **Faith** first not only because of its effect on the spiritual health of each individual, but also for its influence on the spiritual health of the country. What we believe in in our hearts and act out in our lives determines how we treat others, what mores are acceptable in society, what laws we pass to make America the type of country that we want to live in, and how we use our assets to make this a better world. Our forefathers were strong Christian people who wanted to establish a country whereby men were free to practice their religion and the government could not dictate or force any religion on its citizens. Laws were developed based on Christian principles. Ethical behavior was a stalwart of our country's early history. Prayer was important and was public as well as private. In essence, we structured our country to be made up of ethical, moral and impartial leaders and citizens. We, as individuals and as a country, have strayed so far from these concepts that returning to them seems impossible. In my opinion, the only way we will return is through God's intervention. We must pray for this change. We must pray for ethical and moral leaders. We must pray for a change of heart by the citizenry. We must once again submit ourselves to God's will.

Family is next on my list. We have strayed so far from the original concept of family. Most of the influences of our culture today move us away from the closeness and love of the family unit. Our morals allow us to have sexual relations outside of marriage, causing many pregnancies that either end in fatherless families, or worse, aborted babies. Activities outside of the family have become more important than activities within the family. (e.g., soccer practice trumps the evening family dinner.) Marriage itself has been desecrated with men marrying men, and women marrying women. The concept of a man being the head of the household and the woman being the nurturer and glue of the family unit is looked upon as archaic. Family time together has given way to material desires and selfish motives. Without a strong family unit as the basic structure of the American culture, what do we turn to for the stability, fidelity, reliability and support that all of us need as we progress through life? In order to turn this around we must fight for the rights of the family and work tirelessly to promote family structure and values. If America can return to the family unit as being the core of our culture, many of the ills in today's society will be reversed.

The third item on the list, **Freedom,** is being threatened today more than it has been in the history of our country. In the first paragraph of the Declaration of Independence, it refers to the Laws of Nature and Nature's God. These laws entitle people to separate and equal station if the ruling body becomes destructive as to certain unalienable rights. Among these unalienable rights are life, liberty and the pursuit of happiness. This was Jefferson's reasoning for justifying the break from British governance. He felt strongly that the British were "destructive to certain unalienable rights," which then allowed people in the colonies to "separate and equal station." In other words, we could become self-governing.

According to the National Center for Constitutional Studies, when Jefferson talks about "the Laws of Nature and Nature's God" he is basically referring to "the rules of moral conduct implanted by nature in the human mind, forming the proper basis for and being superior to all written laws; the will of God revealed to man through his conscience." We are once again approaching this station in our lives as Americans. Our federal government has moved beyond its original purpose. They are now forcing us to:

- Inject an experimental gene therapy solution (mRNA) into our bodies and calling it a "vaccine."
- Wear masks that have been shown not to prevent the Covid virus from passing through the mask.

- Shut down businesses, schools, and churches under the guise of "safety," while allowing liquor stores and big box stores to remain open.
- Fund a foreign war in Ukraine without the Congress declaring an Act of War against Russia.
- Accept illegal immigrants into our country in the millions at our southern border and to pay for their well-being here in the U.S. as illegal aliens.
- Use the FBI to silence and intimidate political opponents.

The list goes on – the bottom line is that the current government has decided that it can pretty much do whatever it wants regardless of how the citizens of the country feel. We have a coalition of the current federal government, big tech, the media and the elites who have decided they will control what we can do, hear or say. We are approaching a crossroad in the U.S., and if the power of the people is not returned to the people, I am afraid we could face civil war. The 2022 election will be pivotal. If the American people do not send a resounding message to the current administration, things will get worse quickly. Unfortunately, having confidence in the election process is not something that is ubiquitous. If you don't know what I mean by that, just watch the documentary "2000 Mules" by Dinesh D'Souza. It will cause you to seriously doubt that we have control over the election process.

Education is the last of my big four. Our young people are our hope for the future. Although I may sound overly negative concerning where we are headed as a nation, I do believe that our hope is in the young. There are currently many youth organizations that try to mold our future leaders into people of faith and integrity. I believe it starts with private and parochial schools, which includes home schooled children. The curriculum that is followed in most of these schools is one that applauds our founding fathers and provides guidelines for treating others as we want to be treated. Fairness, kindness, honesty, humility, patriotism, trusting in and honoring God – these are the by-products of such a curriculum. It creates good people. Good people create good leaders. Good leaders create good government. Good government fosters a good way of life.

Schools and other groups who foster these same virtues are available for young adults also. Colleges like Hillsdale (MI) College, Benedictine (KS) College, and Franciscan University (OH) lead the way. Organizations like the Fellowship of Catholic University Students (FOCUS), who are on over 200 campuses in more than 40 states in the U.S., allow students on secular campuses an opportunity to learn about Christianity and apply it in their lives. Chris Godfrey's Life Athletes promotes Christianity and pro-marriage family values using pro athletes as examples and mentors. Bob Woodson of the Woodson Center is a civil rights activist who offers The Woodson Center's K-12 black history and character curriculum, which is free. He has done wonders in helping the black community over the years and strongly supports helping black youth succeed in America. There are many organizations such as these who give hope to our future.

Let me briefly mention the next three items I listed. I won't go into a lot of details concerning each:

> **Government** is the next topic, but I don't have too much to add to the comments already made in the Freedom section above about the federal government. My only addition is to make an observation that we must find a way to limit the federal government's control over our lives, and get back to allowing state and local governments to have the most (but limited) authority as it concerns governing our daily lives.
>
> **Exercise and Health** is an area that we can have a drastic effect on if we have the discipline to make changes to our life style. Book after book, video after video, podcast after podcast have been created which give a myriad of recommendations for Americans to become and/or remain healthy. Article after article claims to have an easy, fast and secret formula for you to regain your youthful self and stay healthy. If you boil all of them down to a few words, the solution is found in "diet and exercise." It only makes sense that what you eat becomes your body, and how much you exercise dictates how that body functions. The key ingredient to success in this area of exercise and health is simple: Discipline.

Mass Media is the final topic I identified as being more critical compared to some of the other topics covered in the book. The reason I chose it is due to the great influence the media has on what people think and believe. Unless you have time to investigate every story you read, watch or hear, you end up depending upon the accuracy and truthfulness of the person/organization reporting the story. As you, I'm sure, have come to realize, a story with the same facts will be presented 180 degrees differently by CNN and Fox News. The problem is, how do you determine who is providing the facts and not "spinning" the story to follow a specific narrative? It is so difficult to decipher the truth today. Probably one of the few ways to get an idea as to who is spinning a story and who is not is to go back a few years and see how a story was presented, and then determine what really happened based on what you know today. If management at the media source has not changed over that period of time, then the likelihood that that source is still reporting the truth or spinning it just as they had done years earlier is great (e.g., the Trump/Russia hoax). We need a news source with character and integrity that reports the facts and not personal opinions, desires or agendas. We need a Walter Cronkite.

There are certainly other topics that are important that are not on my "most important" list, but without the three F's (Faith, Family and Freedom) changing, the chance of the other topics having a significant influence in changing America is relatively small. In general, we have made great strides in technology over my lifetime. In many cases that has made our lives better. However, it doesn't matter how great our entertainment or our job situation or our travel capabilities have become, without a fundamental change in faith, family and freedom, we are headed for disaster. Are we each individually willing to do our part to change the three F's in our country?

Chapter 22 – Recommendations

You know, it seems like every generation talks about "the good old days" and has a desire to return to those days. I don't know if it is because those days were really better from a quality of life standpoint (physical, mental and spiritual), or because many of us forget the bad things of the past and only recall the good things! When I was growing up, the older folks looked with disdain on rock & roll, fast cars, "duck tails" and tight jeans. They thought Elvis Presley was the devil. (If he was, then who the heck was Jerry Lee Lewis?) They were certain we were going to kill ourselves and other innocent people with the way we drove our hot cars. They also thought that when we died in that car crash we were going straight to hell because of the way we combed our hair and the way our snug fitting clothes left little to the imagination.

I think it is natural to think things were better when we were growing up compared to current times. Change is not easy for most people, and since the end of World War II we have seen nothing but constant and drastic change. Technology has driven much of this. The relaxation of the moral code is also greatly responsible. Computers touch every part of our lives and have opened up avenues to practically anything we are interested in exploring, both honorable and dishonorable. This, I believe, is where my growing up years' wisdom trumps today's.

As I have mentioned early and often in this book, sacrifice, discipline, unselfishness and accountability were emphasized heavily in the 50's and early 60's. These values were not only taught at home, they were also espoused at school, work and church. Growing up, we were surrounded by people (parents, teachers, bosses, pastors) who held us accountable for upholding these values. We weren't always capable of living up to these standards, but we tried very hard to do so and were ashamed when we failed. I don't see that very often today. There are many parents, teachers, bosses and pastors today who themselves do not live up to these values, much less hold the younger generation accountable for doing so. Most people seem to be so into whatever makes them "happy." Too often that "something," in the long run, is not good for you. Drugs, pornography and alcohol are some that come to mind immediately, but there are other stealth items that are almost as denigrating - sports, work, shopping, technology, TV, etc. As many people overdose on these items as people do on drugs, pornography and alcohol. I call them stealth items because they sneak up on you, and before you know it, your whole life centers around one or more of these "un-sinful" things.

I heard it often growing up – "too much of anything is not good for you." We, as a society, have become addicted to not only drugs, sex and alcohol, but also to sports, cell phones, food, and tobacco. Worse yet, there is an element who have become addicted to power and control. Mixing all these things together, we have the recipe for a societal Molotov cocktail. That is where we are today and the explosion is imminent if we don't change our ways.

So, how do we get out of this mess? Unfortunately, I don't believe the current generation is capable of getting out of it. I believe it will literally take an act of God for today's society to change back to a morally based society. That could entail a total economic collapse, a nuclear war, a meteor collision or a truly miraculous event like a spiritual illumination of the conscience – something drastic that will force us to "start over." I think we are beyond having man-made solutions. It will take something catastrophic for people in the U.S. and the world to humble themselves and return to God's ways. I hope I am wrong.

If we are somehow able to survive for a decade or so under the current conditions, I believe the only way to change things for the future is for today's grandparents and parents to influence young children to learn to know God, to love Him, and to keep His commands. I don't think you can start when kids are in their teen years – although we must certainly try. I think you have to start even younger. Kids in their teen years are already extremely influenced by today's culture. Society has made smoking marijuana, being addicted to the computer attached to your hand, not knowing God, and disrespect for life (abortion, suicide, euthanasia, murder) normal.

If you think I am exaggerating, just look at each one of those items separately:

1. Smoking marijuana – State after state in the U.S. is making recreational marijuana legal. If adults can legally get the drug, think how easy it is for young people to get it too. Marijuana has been shown to cause mental health issues in teens, including depression, social anxiety, psychosis, and schizophrenia. (A 2019 study found that 37% of teens had used marijuana.)
2. Mobile device – As far back as 2016 CNN did a poll and found that 50% of all teens felt they were addicted to their mobile device. Think about how much worse that must be today! You practically never see a young person who does not have a cell phone in their hand, regardless of what they are doing. They are constantly checking messages or texting someone or playing games on their phone. Personal interaction has significantly diminished and a teen's life is now lived on their phone. A 2019 study done by Pew Research showed that 60% of teens would rather spend time online with friends than spend time with them in real life. The same study found that 95% of teens have access to smart phones, and 56% connect negative emotions to not having their smart phone with them. There is a connection between increased screen time and depression. Between 2010 and 2015, teenage girls suicides increased by 65%, in direct correlation with increased usage of smart phones (Science Daily). Teens aren't the only ones to be concerned with - 45% of 10-12 year olds actually have smart phones, so we can anticipate more of the same in the future. All of this leads to mental health issues among teens, including anxiety, loneliness, depression and self-absorption.
3. Not knowing God is a more recent phenomenon. Again, in my day if you weren't introduced to God at home, you were more than likely exposed to Him at school - even public schools. Prayer was okay in the classroom at all schools. Every school day was started with the class standing up and holding your hand over your heart, then saying the "Pledge of Allegiance" (including the words "Under God"). "In God We Trust" was on all of our money, Billy Graham was

featured on radio and TV, and Catholic Bishop Fulton J. Sheen's TV program was one of the highest rated shows on television. (There were only three channels back then, so it was hard not to be aware of Bishop Sheen and his show.) Referencing God at work was fine, and pop music included spiritual songs in the Top 10. (The Singing Nuns' "Dominique," a song about St. Dominic, reached No. 1 on the pop charts in 1963; Australia's Sister Janet Mead's "Our Father" reached No. 4 on the pop charts in the U.S. in 1974.)

As you can see, God was no stranger to Americans regardless of the setting or venue. That has drastically changed today. You can't pray in public schools – the U.S. Supreme Court banned school-sponsored prayer in 1962 and anti-religion activists have taken it to the extreme – e.g., a high school football coach was recently fired for taking a knee after football games and privately praying at the 50 yard line. (Fortunately, the Supreme Court of the United States reversed the school's decision saying it violated the coach's First Amendment rights.) Society today is doing all it can to ban God in all phases of our life. So where are youngsters going to get exposed to God if they are unfortunate enough to have parents who do not teach them about Him? And without God, what moral code is being followed by today's young people?

4. The final item is today's disrespect for life. In the 50's and 60's:
    - Abortion was banned
        i. Abortions went from practically 0% to 43% of live births in 1983, then down to 20% in 2019. (In 2019 about 25% of pregnancies in the 15-19 age group ended in abortions) [Note: Fortunately Roe v. Wade was overturned by the Supreme Court this summer (2022), sending the decision back to each individual state's voters to decide.]
    - Suicide was an issue for older adults but not so much for young adults
        i. Overall 8% higher today than in 1950, but for ages 15 – 24 the rate is nearly 300% higher.
    - Euthanasia was something that was unconscionable

- i. Ten states and the District of Columbia have passed laws legalizing assisted suicide today. The numbers of people being euthanized is not large, but it is available in those locations.
- Homicides in the U.S. were less frequent than today
  - i. Homicides are up 15% since 1950 (5.9/100K vs. 5.1/100K).
  - ii. For males ages 15 – 24 the rate today is staggering 20.1/100K.

What are striking are the rates of increase in abortions, suicides and homicides among young adults over my lifetime. Many young people today do not value life. This is a learned behavior. They witness it every day in the U.S. Is pregnancy an inconvenience? No problem; get an abortion. Depressed, lonely, hopeless? No problem; commit suicide. Angry at someone, being disrespected, hate someone? No problem, kill them.

What are some contributing factors to this attitude?
- No moral code
- Living in non-reality with movies, the internet and violent video games
- Watching others do bad things to people and not be held accountable
- Using drugs
- The learned "what's in it for me" attitude

It is no wonder that mental health issues are one of the most serious problems we face in the future. Young people have nowhere to turn, since they have no "faith life" to fall back on. They have no hope, since God and the next life are not relevant to them.

How do we take on this enormous task to turn things around? <u>One soul at a time.</u>

1. We must change ourselves and live a life of virtue.

2. We must reach out to another person and help influence them to do the same when we see them going down a path of darkness.
3. We must become mentors for the young and role models for those who observe what we do and how we do it.
4. We must get involved and share our gifts with others so that through our love they will see that life is special - that it is a wonderful gift from God to be celebrated.

If people see that through discipline, ethical behavior, sacrifice, and trust in God we have attained happiness, maybe they will realize that the world's formula for happiness, i.e., sex, drugs, money, fame, materialism, etc., only leads to heartache and loneliness. They can regain a sense of purpose and become contributors themselves to "The Great Turn-Around."

As my good friend Charlie Johnston, founder of the Corps of Renewal and Charity (CORAC) tells us - we all need to take responsibility for what we did in the past to create this darkness. He fervently counsels us to take three actions in order to live our faith well:

1. Acknowledge God
2. Take the Next Right Step
3. Be a Sign of Hope to Those Around Us

I invite you to join me in following Charlie's guidance and also join me in attempting to bring America back to its founding principles. For a start, here is a prayer I wrote about 40 years ago and have prayed every morning since then. It puts things into perspective at the start of each new day for me:

Lord, as this <u>day begins</u>, so too I begin anew, to bring You into the lives of all those that I touch.

Let my <u>actions today</u> transmit Your love for man, for there are so few today who dare to be gentle, compassionate and loving, yet, still strong enough to stand up for what is right, just and good.

As my <u>day progresses</u>, give me the strength to remain kind, when I am tired of being kind; to hold out my hand to those in need, when my hand is already weary; and to give, when I thought myself to have been previously emptied.

And when <u>evening arrives</u>, help me to have brought as much peace to Your people as Your summer sunsets bring; as much happiness as Your first winter's snow; and as much joy as Your spring warmth.

And as I lay down to <u>rest for the night</u>, with Your help, I will have made this a better world, one day closer to Your Kingdom. Amen.

****

Looking back on my life – God, Prayer, Family - they all played huge roles in bringing peace and happiness into most of my days. Yes, times were simpler back in my growing up days. Technology has sped us up significantly. But even in these tumultuous times, we can strive to right the course and attempt to get "back in the game," so to speak. We need to be God's hands and feet to help make this happen.

Basketball has always been a large part of my life, so it would only be appropriate for me to end this book with a basketball analogy. Remember, God will do His part to get us back in the game if we but ask Him. For our part, let's take a lesson from a free throw shooter who is in the heat of a basketball game. Let's review his/her shooting principles and apply those principles to our lives. Let each of us:

1. Slow down and take a couple of deep breaths
2. Focus on the goal
3. Establish a balanced stance and relax
4. Execute with confidence
5. Follow through

With God's help, we can get "back in the game" – one point at a time.

About the Author

Joe Brickner grew up in Ohio in an industrial town in the northwestern part of the state. His family was not well-to-do, but he was able to attend college anyway by earning a basketball scholarship to St. Benedict's College (now Benedictine College) in Atchison, Kansas. After graduating with a math degree, he pursued a business career with Southwestern Bell Telephone Company (now AT&T).

While working at Bell he was able to earn an MBA from Southern Illinois University and a Doctor of Management degree from Webster University in St. Louis. These degrees were instrumental in his having the opportunity to retire from his corporate executive position at the age of 50 to become a college professor and Benedictine's head men's basketball coach. He coached for 12 years and continued teaching full time for another two years. He then became the CFO for a small drug development company. After retiring for the third time, he wrote his first book called, "So, You want to be a Coach..." The book is about his drastic career change and what it is like to actually coach from the bench instead of from the stands!

Dr. Brickner's book spawned a podcast called *"Building with Brick – Foundational Wisdom on Coaching, Careers and Christ."* The weekly podcast can most easily be found by going to Dr. Brickner's website, https://www.drjoebrickner.com, and choosing the video or audio podcast menu choice.

After a successful first book, Joe decided to write a serious reflection of how America has changed over his lifetime. His latest book, "America: Lost in Place" is both a nostalgic recollection and a thought provoking initiative that will cause readers to pause and consider just where we are headed in today's America. His conclusions and recommendations will strike a nerve with most Americans.

Dr. Brickner currently lives in KC with his wife of nearly 40 years, Connie. And yes, he is still playing basketball at 70+.

Other Offerings from the Author

As a result of writing his first book, "So, You want to be a Coach...," Dr. Brickner created a weekly podcast where he interviews athletic role models. The podcast is called:

"Building with Brick: Foundational Wisdom on Coaching, Careers and Christ"

The video and audio podcast links can be found at www.drjoebrickner.com.

www.ingramcontent.com/pod-product-compliance
Lightning Source LLC
Chambersburg PA
CBHW061441040426
42450CB00007B/1148